Teaching At-Risk Students
in the K-4 Classroom:
Language, Literacy, Learning

Teaching At-Risk Students in the K-4 Classroom: Language, Literacy, Learning

Carole F. Stice

and

John E. Bertrand, Eds.

1999

Christopher-Gordon Publishers, Inc.
Norwood, Massachusetts

Credits

Every effort has been made to contact copyright holders for permission to reproduce borrowed material where necessary. We apologize for any oversights and would be happy to rectify them in future printings.

All student work used with permission.

The Bill Harp Professional Teachers's Library
An Imprint of
Christopher-Gordon Publishers, Inc.
1502 Providence Highway, Suite #12
Norwood, MA 02062
(800) 934-8322

Printed in the United States of America

10 9 8 7 6 5 4 3 2

04 03 02 01 00

Library of Congress Catalog Card Number: 99-66213
ISBN: 0-926842-99-4

In memory of

Pat Tefft Cousin

and for

Middle Tennessee TAWL Members

and

all the other reflective, caring teachers

from whom we have learned so much.

Thank you.

Carole F. Stice
John E. Bertrand

Acknowledgements

The editors wish to acknowledge the help and encouragement of Sue Canavan, Senior Editor at Christopher-Gordon, Publishers. Without her confidence in the value of these stories, they never would have left middle Tennessee. And we wish to thank Nancy P. Bertrand for her painstaking editing and insightful recommendations with each of the chapters.

Table Of Contents

Preface

Teaching and teachers are under constant criticism, it seems. Politicians promise to become the "education" senator, govenor, president, etc., and put an end to all the nation's schooling difficulties. Newspaper and journal articles lambaste one or another aspect of education. Test scores are said to show that U. S. schools do not compete well internationally. And yet, the U. S. still leads the world in technology and innovation. Partly, that condition is due to good teachers.

We each remember favorite and remarkable teachers who may have turned our lives around. This book was written to remind us that those teachers are still here. They exist, embattled though they may be, in every school in the country, molding children's hearts and minds, helping young people prepare for the future, and helping direct or redirect lives, just as they always have.

This book provides an opportunity for a handful of such teachers to tell their stories. It was written for prospective and beginning early elementary grade teachers, especially those who work with large numbers of high risk students. It was also written for veteran teachers who desire to read about other teachers like themselves and for teachers in need of reassurance that they can and do make a positive difference in the lives of their students. It was written for teachers who are looking for a few good ideas and a lot of inspiration.

The book may also serve as a resource for administrators interested in examples of reflective teaching in learner-centered classrooms and for parents, especially parents of children at risk, to help them identify the kinds of classrooms they may want for their children. In this book the reader will meet six unique, learning and kid-friendly, knowledgeable, reflective teachers who are a credit to the profession.

Chapters 1 through 6 are about a diverse kindergarten, a rural first grade, an inner city second grade, a small town third grade, a fourth grade in a special school for learning disabled children, and a multi-age ESL classroom, respectively. The writers have provided us with in-depth looks into their highly successful, literacy and content rich classrooms focusing on children at risk of school failure. These classrooms are scattered across four school districts in middle Tennessee.

The writers allow us into their thought processes as they come to know the characteristics, and plan for the needs of individual students. They share with us several child language and learning stories as well as some of their struggles and aspirations. Chapters 7 and 8 depart from classroom story telling. Chapter 7 recounts how two parent/school coordinators established highly successful programs against overwhelming odds, one in an inner city community and the other in an impovrished rural school district in Appalachia. The similarities between these two people and the two extremely different yet effective programs they created provide insights into what is necessary for developing successful parent/school partnership programs anywhere. Finally, Chapter 8 provides a brief account of the major issues in the current debate about early literacy instruction, drawing from information about reading and writing, issues explored in the preceding chapters, and recent research summaries.

Introduction

The teachers described in the following chapters are examples of empowered, caring, reflective practitioners. They know children, language development, and how to create rich, diverse learning opportunities for students. None of these teachers teach in ideal situations. Rather, they live in places where there is great effort exerted to control what teachers do. A major emphasis in each of their school districts is on higher test scores, whether that supports good teaching and learning or not.

These teachers resist such pressures as well as they can, focusing on what they know to be good pedagogy and trying to provide resources and environmental conditions they believe will best promote real, lasting, and important learning. They share among themselves, as major teaching and learning goals, the fostering in their students of creative self-expression, caring for themselves and for each other, independence, self-confidence based on real accomplishment, critical thinking, and curiosity about, as well as concern for, the world in which we live.

Slavin (1989) defines "at-risk" as referring to students of normal intelligence who are failing to acquire the basic skills necessary for success in school and later life. Low-income children are considered to be most at risk for school and later life failures. But many other characteristics jeopardize learning and school achievement for students.

There have always been children who do not thrive in schools, and children who do not learn to read and write well are considered to be most at risk. Focusing on how reflective teachers successfully work with difficult, struggling children provides insight into how good teachers manage the miracles they seem to accomplish. These teachers, and others like them, rarely if ever employ teacher's manuals, teach to-the-test, mechanically follow mandated skills lists, use programmed instruction, or subject their students to instructional gimmicks and surface level, rote learning. They agree that such practices are not good for children, and their promotion has hurt children, teaching, and teachers.

Rather, they believe in and support helping children learn to read, write, and think for themselves. (Dressman, McCarty, & Benson, 1998; Fountas, & Pinnell,1996). We, the editors, believe in and support helping teachers read, learn, and think for themselves. We believe that what is needed is greater local control and more teachers who see themselves as people with a calling to teach, rather than merely curriculum overseers and taskmasters.

The classrooms described in these pages are each unique learning environments. They are places where the teacher and the children together have created a family of learners with their own interests and designs. Although third graders, for example, still learn multiplication facts and cursive handwriting, much of the curriculum is determined by what the children find compelling. The question is, what does the teacher do to scaffold literacy onto those interests as the children talk, listen, read, write, and think in new and increasingly complex ways?

The classrooms described in this book serve many children typically considered to be at risk; children living in poverty, some with learning disabilities of various kinds, some who do not speak English yet, and some who have been identified as having various psychological and emotional problems. However, over time, these children less and less exhibit the limited learning that corresponds with such at-risk factors. If these classrooms were to be tested with a national test, squashed into the cookie cutter format of a state or national curriculum, or otherwise altered, would that improve them in any way? We think not. These classrooms and countless others like them need to be protected from such overcontrol. Rather, all teachers need to be more empowered, reflective, encouraged to be more informed about the nature of learning, literacy, and children's development. They need to use that information and their own inspiration to be responsive to the particular students they have.

Good classrooms and good schools provide experiences that promote a love of learning. They also provide opportunities for learners to explore and experiment with their own inquiry pursuits with teacher support and within whatever the general focus of study happens to be. Good schools value children and promote a curriculum which provides meaningful learning experiences rich in resources and content, high in standards, guided by caring, thoughtful, often passionate, and always knowledgeable and reflective teachers.

From such classrooms come the stories of the children in this book. These success stories are ultimately about the power of reflective, learner-centered teaching that reaches and saves difficult children. But even more, these stories are about teachers who know how to create families or communities of learners in their classrooms. They are teachers who remember why they chose teaching in the first place and who still instruct with passion. Today, perhaps more than ever before, the value and importance of good teachers and good teaching should not be overestimated, must not be undervalued, cannot be replaced by technology, and should not be controlled by programs and misguided accountability measures.

Reflective, caring teachers help their students develop confidence in themselves as capable people. They help their students experience hope for a safe and successful future in what for many young people is an all too frightening and hopeless world. They establish the values of kindness, sharing, caring, and perseverance at a time in our society when those attributes are too seldom seen in schools. The wonderful teaching found in these and other such classrooms should be encouraged and supported.

We hope teachers, parents, and administrators will search out their own examples of reflective, caring teachers in language and content rich learning communities within their schools: learn about them, learn from them, and find ways to help new teachers emulate them in tenor and style. And we fervently hope society recognizes the need to protect and defend good teachers and their classrooms—for regrettably they are an endangered species.

Chapter 1

"We Teached Ourselves": Good Beginnings in a Diverse Kindergarten

Linda Edwards

A few years ago, I decided to take a pottery class. I knew nothing about pottery except that I liked it and thought I wanted to try my hand, so to speak, at a craft. I also wanted to try learning something absolutely new to remind myself what it's like. It was not a pleasant experience, partly because I had a family crisis during that time, and partly because the teacher was not accustomed to teaching people who knew nothing about her particular art form. Those two facts made me an at-risk learner. That is, I came to the process with little or no prior knowledge and in my case, no discernible talent. I also had personal problems that got in the way of regular attendance and hence of my learning. There were many things she could have done to help me, but she didn't do them, either because she did not know what to, or because she could not/would not take the time. Had I not been an adult with my own purpose and solid ego structure, I would have quit long before I did.

Children at risk of school failure are part of every kindergarten class I teach. I first began to explore instructional alternatives to the traditional methods I'd been taught as an undergraduate when I realized that a typical reading readiness program with its emphasis on letters, sounds, and visual discrimination did not seem to meet the needs of many of my students. By each year's end, many students recognized less than half the letters of the alphabet, couldn't discriminate between two similar shapes, designs, or words, and knew very few sound-letter correspondences. These children did not seem markedly less intelligent then their peers; in fact, they usually brought "life skills" to school that their more successful counterparts often lacked.

While the most obviously at-risk children enter school with too few experiences that connect to the world of the classroom, others seem to bring considerable funds of knowledge about the world but lack fine visual discrimination experiences or the extensive language and linguistic skills necessary for easy success with school learning. Still others appear at risk because they lack the social and interpersonal abilities that enable them to learn from and engage successfully in group activities during this first year of "real school". In addition, a common thread among most at-risk students is that they tend to possess learning style strengths that are not the main focus of more typical instructional methods that are geared primarily toward visual learning. A curriculum which contains a strong oral language component and includes many opportunities for movement and active involvement builds on auditory and kinesthetic strengths without penalizing children who are more visual.

Another common trait among kindergartners who are at-risk is that they lack confidence in their own abilities. Vygotsky's social learning theory with its "zone of proximal development" (Vygotsky, 1978), suggests that what a child can accomplish with help today, she can do on her own tomorrow. As I discovered in the course of my teaching, at risk learners generally need more support and help early on than other children. Sometimes they require just a vote of confidence. Sometimes they need to be talked through a process one more time. Sometimes they need to work with another student for a while (all interventions from which I too could have benefited in that pottery class).

When activities are meaningful to the learner, children almost always want to participate, especially when the necessary scaffolding is available. Providing support allows such children to develop control over their own learning; optimally they are empowered by a learning environment which allows them to work at their own pace and level without penalizing them for who they are. While many at-risk children lag behind their peers in developmental literacy and numeracy, they often excel in subject areas that involve hands-on learning. Perhaps more than other children, at-risk learners require activities which directly relate current topics of study to their prior knowledge. In this way they are able to make sense for themselves of their in school experiences.

During a recent unit on dinosaurs, for instance, we read *Maia: A Dinosaur Grown Up*, (Horner & Gorman, 1985). I read it to the children one chapter a day. We used a yardstick to draw Maia's length at birth. The children made their own Maias and used them to locate and record things in our classroom that were both longer and shorter than Maia, the dinosaur. We also dramatized each chapter after reading it to help students internalize the story's sequence of events (see Paley, 1981).

Before the unit began, we made a list of dinosaur facts and a list of what we wanted to learn about dinosaurs to guide our study. We read dinosaur poems, sang dinosaur songs, pretended to be our favorite dinosaurs, and read both fiction and non-fiction books about dinosaurs. As our unit progressed, we charted newly acquired information, and they recorded newly found facts they wanted to remember in learning logs. They expanded their knowledge through art, music, and movement.

The more aware I became of the developmental issues involved in young children's emerging and early literacy and numeracy, the more I was dissatisfied. Basing changes on professional readings, information gathered at professional meetings, suggestions from colleagues, and insights garnered from university classes, I began to alter the way my classroom and my curriculum were structured. Among the most influential works was Brian Cambourne's *The Whole Story* (1988) and his conditions of natural learning.

This book served as a framework to guide the planning and implementing of a classroom environment that could utilize the abilities and highlight the strengths all my kindergartners bring to school. Today, I immerse students in literacy learning opportunities and provide daily demonstrations of the skills and strategies they need. I expect each student to be successful, and I try to respond in ways that support all their attempts at reading and writing. I accept their approximations and gradually teach new skills and strategies in the context of the books, poems, and songs we read, as well as the stories, labels, lists, and so on that we write. I look for evidence of growth over time rather than expecting every student to acquire every skill and concept or internalize every strategy immediately. I hold them responsible for their own learning and for using the skills and strategies we are exploring as they engage in the meaningful learning taking place in our classroom. To these ends I remind, suggest, group, encourage, explain, model, question, tease, play, praise, refuse to do for them what they can do for themselves, and employ a host of other techniques.

While I always read to them several times a day, I did not always have my students write as much as I do now. Exploring writing with emergent readers is a major avenue for linking the interpersonal to literacy development through authentic reading and writing activities. From the first day of school, students are encouraged to write about their interests and experiences in their journals.

Mechanics and conventions of print are modeled daily prior to letting them do their own writing.

Students' writing moves from scribbling and making letter-like marks, to drawing, labeling their drawings, writing short nearly readable phrases, and finally to writing readable sentences as they come gradually to understand more about spelling, spacing, features of print, and the other requirements for putting ideas on paper that others can read. Children at risk are often especially interested in writing. Being able to write about topics that are personally relevant validates their efforts and their lives and provides successes for those children who may already be questioning their own academic potential. This is partly because success is its own reward and partly because all children have interesting events and insights to share. Through writing, I am able to help each child create a personal niche within the classroom community.

Many conditions place young children at risk in school. That there is more than one cause for concern is clear. For some children, school is just so different from home that transition is difficult. *Ari* is the third child of an Israeli family who immigrated to the United States so his father could teach at a local university. He is not a child most people would think of as being at risk, yet he certainly was. The youngest child in his family and the youngest son of two boys, Ari has been sheltered from contact with the outside world. His rather introverted and bookish family do not have many social contacts, and Ari is completely inexperienced at being part of a group of peers. Before school started, Ari's mother warned me that "Ari is not like my other two children", but she was not specific and so nothing really prepared me for how different Ari would actually be.

Although he had attended a local preschool, he had not yet learned to relate to and play with other children. During the first few weeks of kindergarten, I observed several behaviors that seemed to indicate some kind of communication disorder, but I was not qualified to render a more specific analysis. Ari's productive language was minimal. He also seemed unaware of situations in which he could/should interact with others. His responses to direct questions often echoed exactly what was said to him. If I asked him, "Would you like to play with the blocks?", Ari would answer, "You would like to play with the blocks."

While his unusual syntax was puzzling, Ari was already a fluent reader who would often begin reading aloud whatever caught his eye during group activities or shared book. His parents feared any kind of label that might result in his being taken out of the regular education program and placed in a class for students with language or other disabilities. They were not receptive to having him tested to determine if there were known ways to approach his learning, nor was our school psychologist inclined to test kindergarten students so early in the year. Therefore, I developed my own list of kindergarten objectives for Ari.

Academics were not the issue since he was already reading and doing math far above kindergarten levels. My goals for Ari were to help him learn to interact in positive ways with his peers and to improve his oral English language skills. Ari had real difficulty coping with even small changes in class routines. Field trips and class parties were frightening events and upset him dreadfully. I hoped to help him learn to negotiate unfamiliar situations and events without anxiety and to voice his needs rather than waiting expectantly for someone else to "know" what he wanted.

Ari had a computer at home and knew the software in our classroom at least as well as I did. After a few months of school, I realized that part of the problem was that he was so mesmerized by the computer he wanted very little social contact with real children, especially during center time if he was allowed to be at the computer.

The Physical Education teacher told me that Ari just stood and stared at the sky or walked around in circles by himself when he was at PE. Since it was obvious that Ari did not know how to initiate play with his peers and possibly was not even aware of their existence much of the time, I assigned a different child each day to play with Ari. During the course of the day, the designated child was responsible for sitting with Ari at lunch and snack time, bringing him to centers, and involving him in playing outside. Over the course of the year, Ari gradually learned to play with the other children in this class and his expressive language became more nearly age appropriate. In fact, by the end of the year, he was so social that he sometimes got angry when I insisted that he finish a task before going to play with his friends. I knew he was going to be all right when I finally began seeing him assert himself with his peers in play and other group situations.

Different from Ari, but also at risk, *Thomas* lives in an inner city housing project. Although I had him two years ago, he still comes by to see me on a regular basis so I know how he is doing. When he started school, he functioned in most ways like a three-year-old. His mother, who had not yet completed high school, was the single parent of two boys and constantly struggling to make ends meet. She was very concerned about Thomas' education and wanted him to do well. There was considerable extended family nearby so Thomas was often with his grandmother, aunts, uncles and cousins. Consequently, he brought a rich sense of belonging and connectedness to school.

An initial assessment of Thomas' academic skills indicated that he recognized no colors, shapes, letters, or numbers. He did not recognize his name in print, and he could not write it. He enjoyed hands-on activities which allowed movement and talking, but was easily distracted and often disruptive in group situations where he had to share and negotiate his own participation. Thomas often got in trouble on the school bus, in the cafeteria, and in the library where sitting still and being quiet are valued, needed, and expected. He could usually tell me what he should have done after an infraction, but it took several months of school before he was able to reign in his natural, boisterous impulsiveness sufficiently to follow the rules. If someone had not intervened in kind and caring ways, that might still be the case.

A quick analysis of Thomas' learning preferences indicated that he was a highly auditory and kinesthetic learner from a culture where physical prowess is valued and auditory stimuli are almost constant. It was not surprising, therefore, that Thomas' visual perception and acuity lagged behind the fine development of his other senses since he had not had much experience with books, paper, crayons, pencils, scissors, glue, or reading and writing prior to starting school.

Figure 1.1   Thomas' scribble

Writing time gave Thomas the impetus to master the conventions of print, letter recognition, and sound/letter correspondences. He was quick to pick up on my invitations to write about his life outside of school. He was among the first to realize that I wanted him to write like I did in our daily modeled writing focus lessons. Every day, he could hardly wait to write about his adventures with his friends and cousins. Writing connected the affective to the cognitive to the tactile for Thomas.

The first letters Thomas learned were those in his name and in his friends' names. From early on, he could tell me the sounds he wanted to represent, but he was unaware of any possible letters that might spell them. Using a sound/symbol correspondence card, I helped Thomas make the connection between letters and sounds, focusing at first on initial letter sounds only. If he wanted to spell the word "put" for example, I would ask him what sound he heard at the beginning of that word. We would look for the corresponding word—in this case "p" for pig. Then he would write that letter, etc. He learned more letters through spelling significant words for his own writing than he ever would have through drill with flash cards or on such abstract activities as worksheets.

Figure 1. 2   Thomas' Writing

It took a while for Thomas' interest in letters and sounds in his writing to carry over into his reading. At the end of the year, his social behaviors were still often inappropriate, and he did not recognize all of the letters of the alphabet when presented out of order. He had excellent comprehension of books read aloud and was doing well in math, probably because it was taught almost exclusively through real, functional opportunities in the classroom to count, measure, and estimate, as well as through manipulative activities which related concrete experiences to abstract concepts.

During a conference with Thomas' mother, I suggested that a second year in kindergarten would give him opportunity to mature physically and emotionally and to develop more academic skills and confidence so that first grade would not be such a struggle. She told me that Thomas was really happy in kindergarten, that she had not realized how much he needed to learn in just one year and that she wanted him to stay in my class because, "I understood him".

Thomas' second year of kindergarten gave him a chance to be a leader and an expert rather than a follower who had to rely on others for assistance. He was an adept peer tutor at the computer and in math learning centers. His reading often utilized language structures and meaning cues, but still failed to take sufficient notice of sound-letter patterns. To move beyond emergent reading, he had to learn to override his impulsive, intuitive approach to learning, his drive to personalize and make sense of his experiences and leap to connections without adequate data. He had to slow down long enough to take into account printed symbols and the sounds they represented as he saw them on the page. I also knew that it was especially important to praise Thomas' successful use of two language cueing systems before attempting to direct him to reconsider another. For instance, one day when Thomas saw "I read about spaceships . . ." on the page, he said, "I read about rockets . . ." The picture looked like a rocket. I said something like, "Is that word 'rocket'?", and Thomas answered, "No, because it doesn't start with an 'r'," a response I found amazing. We spent a lot of time talking about letter-sounds, and I told him often what good thinking and good reading he was doing.

Eventually, using simple caption books, predictable books, short poems, and other similar materials, Thomas learned to use his growing store of knowledge about sound-letter relationships in reading although they had been in place for some time in his writing.

PaulRonteze KYE

MOlïiO

WT z̃ ZOO

and saw G f

FoxɔrDɔpK.

*Paul, Ronteze, Kyle and
Mario went to the zoo and
saw a giraffe, a fox, a cat
and a duck.*

Figure 1.3 A piece of writing from early in Thomas' second year of kindergarten.

When Thomas went to first grade, we continued our close relationship. He still had occasional problems with self-control, so my classroom was often a place he could come to for a mini-counseling session. During one such visit, I could not stop immediately to talk to him, so I asked him to write about what had happened and what he would do when he went back to class. The unconditional acceptance he finds in my room apparently serves as a kind of anchor for him at school, and I enjoy knowing him and watching him grow and develop.

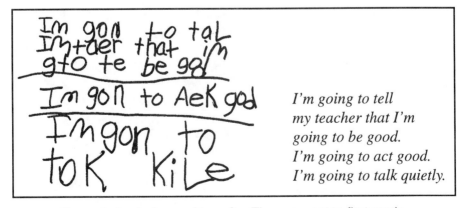

Im gon to tal
Imtäer that im
gto te be ggl
Im gon to AeK god
Im gon to
toK KiLe

*I'm going to tell
my teacher that I'm
going to be good.
I'm going to act good.
I'm going to talk quietly.*

Figure 1. 4   A piece written after Thomas went to first grade.

Charlie is the middle child in a family of three boys. Even at age five, he was exceptionally athletic and seemed to be in perpetual motion. Unfortunately, being the youngest of three sons born in rapid succession to parents who believed that "boys will be boys", especially theirs, had created in Charlie the idea that he had to do outrageous things in order to be noticed. At school, he was very aggressive, hitting, kicking, biting, and pushing. There was a constant stream of complaints from the parents of my other students about Charlie's infractions. Although his academic skills lagged far behind those of most of the other children, getting his social behavior under control took precedent. I knew he wouldn't learn much, and neither would anyone else, if he couldn't control his aggressive and anti-social actions.

Charlie lacked confidence in himself as a person and as a learner. Even though some of the simplest tasks were difficult for him, I always tried to give him enough support so that he could experience success. Because of his middle child status, Charlie had rarely had much one-on-one time with adults. What he really needed was nurturing. He needed to know that he could get help and positive attention if and when he wanted it. He also needed to learn to struggle with a task that was difficult without giving up in frustration.

At first, it was necessary to station myself, a parent volunteer, or a more proficient student by Charlie to keep him on task. As time went by, he needed less and less help once he got started. I discovered that it was more important to accept whatever Charlie could do and gradually shape his work into more desirable forms than to be at all critical of his initial efforts. Hearing that I was proud of how hard he was working seemed to give him a new lens though which to view himself. The quality of his work improved drastically once he realized he was capable and that his efforts would be recognized and praised.

The first breakthroughs in Charlie's behavior came during activity times when he "had important work to do." Because he had not developed the ability to interact constructively with his peers, other students' parents tended to villanize Charlie. Some parents instructed their children to stay away from him. Helping the rest of the class see Charlie as a potential friend became important. This process began with my pointing out Charlie's positive qualities and acceptable behaviors. At first, occasions for praise were few and far between, but once I adopted a policy of catching Charlie being good and pointing it out, the other children in the class began noticing the positive changes in Charlie's behavior and commenting on them. "Mrs. Edwards, did you notice how nicely Charlie was standing in line in the cafeteria?" "Charlie, it was really nice of you to help me find my lunch box."

The children's awareness of and comments on Charlie's behavior set a new and higher standard of caring for everyone in class. Most importantly, news of the "new" Charlie also filtered home to parents and Charlie's image improved throughout our classroom and extended family community. But Charlie's aggressive behavior had created discord, if not pure havoc, in our classroom early in the year. The rest of the children learned important lessons about speaking up for themselves. As a group, we worked to help each other be more assertive and express feelings about inappropriate behavior to the person doing it rather than running to the teacher and always expecting me to intervene.

Each time Charlie went to "time out" to calm down after an incident with another child, analyzing the situation afterwards was a priority. He and I always talked about what he had done, what he should have done, and what he would do the next time. Early in the year, Charlie often had trouble stating what his offense had been. Soon, we were spending more time on what Charlie should have done and his plans for, and committment to, making better choices next time. I recognized real progress for a six-year-old when Charlie could tell me what he had done and what he would do next time. And eventually, the two came together so that he could stop his problem behavior before he did it and do what he had learned was the appropriate thing for being with other children and being in a classroom.

Awareness of other, more appropriate behavior options was the beginning of Charlie's journey into self-control. While he certainly was not perfectly behaved at the end of kindergarten, Charlie had changed from an aggressive, completely ego driven child no one liked into a sensitive, caring child who valued his place in our classroom family. Ultimately, Charlie did well at our school. At the end of fourth grade when he was leaving to go to middle school, Charlie's mom came by to thank me for "making such a difference" with Charlie. He had become a good student with many friends. He was still himself, athletic and energetic, but he was also confident and in control of himself and as a result, in control of his school learning.

Marina is the youngest daughter of Bosnian immigrant parents. I learned that her family left Bosnia with very few personal possessions shortly after her birth to come to America through sponsorship by a local church group. I communicated primarily with her father who spoke limited English; her mother smiled pleasantly but never spoke when I saw her. By contrast, Marina spoke English confidently and virtually without accent. She was affectionate and very sociable. She was well-dressed and always had the things she needed for school as soon as I asked for them. Marina's parents obviously cared deeply for her. The problem was that they were unable to reinforce the school skills with which Marina struggled because of their own limited English and the all consuming effort it took to make a new life in America.

Marina's excellent English indicated that she was an auditory learner. Marina especially enjoyed thematically-based instruction. Though she internalized many of the literacy skills she learned during our theme related activities, she needed meaningful contexts to help her make sense of the skills and concepts she was trying to learn. One of her favorite choices during reading time was reading the charts of familiar songs and poems we have posted around the classroom. Even though she still did not recognize the alphabet out of order, she could pick out words she could read from all the print resources available in the environment. Marina would sit for long periods of time and "partner read" the small books introduced during guided reading times with her friends. Learning was an intensely social activity for her. She relied on her friends' proficiency to fill in the gaps in her own. Apprentice-like, Marina scaffolded her own learning onto theirs, instinctively knowing what and who would provide the best source of assistance.

Although she had not acquired as many skills as some of her peers by the end of the year, she had internalized many understandings about print and how to read and write. She developed enough confidence to attempt and to persist at difficult tasks because she was supported by her friends. I did not teach Marina nearly as much as her friends did, but she had made enough progress to be successful in first grade. Even with little academic support at home in terms of her parents working with her, they clearly supported her school learning. They provided her with supplies, came to all school functions, tried to give her help at home, listened to my suggestions, and were visibly proud of her achievements.

Although most parents, I think, care about their children's learning, they do not all demonstrate the pride in accomplishment that Marina's parents showed her. *Suzanne* is an example of a child who did not receive enough attention and support at home. Suzanne is the youngest of three girls. Her parents were divorced, and she rarely saw her father. Her mother was consumed with completing her doctoral work at a local university and had little time for Suzanne and her sisters. Suzanne's older sisters who had had a more stable family structure at Suzanne's age coped better with their lives than did Suzanne. Often left with teenaged caregivers, Suzanne floundered. A highly affectionate child, but flighty and easily distracted at school, Suzanne was bright and quick to learn. She was also very impulsive. It was hard for her to see other children do inappropriate things without joining in. The key to Suzanne's success in school was to help her accept responsibility for her own behavior and learn to stay focused amidst distractions.

At the beginning of the year, Suzanne could never find her belongings in our classroom. Finishing even the simplest task proved difficult because she spent most of each center period talking to children seated nearby, rather than completing her own work. When the year began, she recognized no letters and could not write her name. However, she was eager to learn. Suzanne had a short attention span and was easily frustrated, but frequent reminders about what she should be doing (hands in lap, eyes on the book), helped her keep focused. Relentless insistence that she put her things away, clean up her work space, and finish her center tasks eventually paid off. Suzanne learned to stay on task during group time and at centers, and she learned to start and finish a job in the time allotted. Many redirection cues reminding her to look at me or at her paper, to put her hands in her lap, to pick up her pencil, and to write were required and seemed to help. Drawing attention to other children's appropriate behavior (and then gently correcting Suzanne) usually gave her opportunities to correct herself before I intervened more directly. Noticing Suzanne as soon as her behavior was appropriate gave her the positive reinforcement she needed for her choices in our classroom.

By November, Suzanne completed most tasks with only a little assistance from me. She recognized most letters and wrote her name easily and well. She was usually able to sit quietly and listen during a group activity and rarely got into trouble outside the classroom. She learned to get right to work immediately so that she could choose something afterward that she wanted to do before time was up. All Suzanne needed was kind, but firm insistence that she conform to expectations coupled with recognition and appreciation for the good choices she made. Her unstructured home life had not taught her to resist impulses and distractions, but she took obvious pride in new accomplishments at school and so did I.

The children I have described have been some of my most obviously at-risk students, but very few children come to school without some issues and conditions that lead to difficulties. All children have periods during which they are potentially at risk. It is up to teachers to read the signs, assess the problems, and help children develop effective strategies for overcoming stumbling blocks to successful school learning. Yet this often presents considerable challenge. The need to deal constructively with *Joshua*, a child who cried everyday for weeks when he first started kindergarten, taxed my abilities to their fullest. Every afternoon, Joshua wet his pants in an attempt to go home early to his mother and new baby sister. One day, in the midst of the day's pants wetting and hysterical episode, I asked him why he acted like that. He replied, wailing, "Because I want my Mommy." I said, "Well, I'm sure she wants you too, but I bet she doesn't stand in the middle of the floor screaming and wet her pants." Joshua stopped crying instantly and thought about that. I suppose the picture of his mother wetting her pants was so absurd and embarrassing that is why he never threw another tantrum again in our classroom.

Usually, tantrums are connected with insistence that students perform some school task they do not want to do. School is often the very first time that many children have been asked to do something they do not want to do. The sheer variability of children's behaviors also stretches a teacher's knowledge and abilities to respond in positive ways. When I think of unusual behaviors, I remember *Sonja*. Sonja only talked when she was supposed to listen. It was as though she had exactly confused the two. Her favorite time to talk was during read aloud. I had to keep Sonja next to me and promise to spend a few minutes talking to her after book sharing time to help her begin to learn when to talk and when to listen.

Working with and caring for unique personality characteristics is all part of living in an active and successful classroom. Much of what allows the children and me to live together and form a community of learners and friends is the predictable nature of our day. Our daily routine is well established by the end of the second week of school. It is posted in both pictorial form and printed on a schedule or task management board. The schedule, in a pocket chart with movable cards, allows for any daily variations we need or want to make. Providing a stable environment for children, as well as a literacy and content rich one, is important. Also, some children do not adapt well to even slight changes, and they need to know what will happen next during the school day. Since I began using the pocket chart schedule, I have noticed that many of my students will change the schedule cards to reflect what we are doing if I forget to do it.

We begin each day with calendar activities and assemble our pocket schedule chart for the day. A fifteen to twenty minute large group language activity involving reading poems or songs on charts, a big book, or a piece of children's literature is followed by forty-five minutes of language arts learning centers, allowing students time for independent practice of language skills. A fifteen to twenty minute large group math activity using manipulatives, and/or a piece of children's literature, to introduce or reinforce a math concept precedes a thirty minute block of math center time during which students explore concepts, and facts previously introduced.

Prior to lunch, there is a five to ten minute read-aloud period. Sometimes, the book or poem shared relates to a theme we are studying. But always, it is a piece to be enjoyed. After lunch, we relax by sharing personal news. The process of recording the children's news on paper in our Class News Book provides demonstrations of a variety of print conventions including left to right, spacing, initial letter sounds, voice print match, and many others. A thirty minute writing period including independent writing and focused group instruction follows. A brief outdoor play period preceeds a twenty to thirty minute activity related to the science and/or social studies theme we are exploring.

Rest time has every child lying quietly on a rest mat, but it evolves during the year into a time for children to finish projects started earlier in the day. By the end of the year, some children are choosing between several independent activities during rest time while others still prefer to really rest. Then the children participate in art, music, and physical education classes for an hour each afternoon. We end the day with another read-aloud period and a simple evaluation of how our day has gone.

Keeping large group times short minimizes behavior problems related to young children not being able to sit still. Activity periods following group instruction give students an immediate opportunity to apply what they have learned in meaningful contexts and provide opportunity for them to be legitimately active after a mainly passive large group lesson. Once children have been taught how to work independently at centers for up to forty-five minutes, I am able to work with individuals and groups.

Good literature ties our day together. Many group activities in all subject areas focus around one or two wonderful picture books. Children are free to read throughout the day, particularly during transition periods. Our classroom routine builds a strong link between reading, writing, and children's personal lives outside the classroom. Students who come with background characteristics placing them at risk usually thrive in my classroom because we establish an environment that values them as individuals and rewards their efforts. They quickly learn that their ideas and abilities are prized, and they relish opportunities to communicate their ideas and experiences to their peers and to me.

Having good resources is essential to good teaching and meeting the needs of all the children. Big books and predictable books suited to the instructional needs of emergent readers build learners' confidence and their crucial self-image as readers. Varied manipulatives for teaching math allow students to develop math concepts as concrete functions and translate those concepts over time to more abstract forms. Materials that encourage personal connections with science, social studies, art, music and movement integrate school experiences with "real" life.

Publishing our own books is a natural outgrowth of our daily writing program. I divide the children into five ability groups for writing so that students with similar needs are working with me at the same time. I work with each writing group once a week while the rest of the class write in their journals. I do not begin this process until most of the children can remember tomorrow what they write today. During a focused writing lesson with a small group, I assist the children with their composing, spelling, and basic punctuation. Later in the year, I help them edit and expand their work as authors. The day after a group has written, they become illustrators and publishers, assembling their books, drawing pictures, and preparing the covers made from pieces of precut wall paper. When illustrations are complete, students share their finished books with the class and place them in the class library.

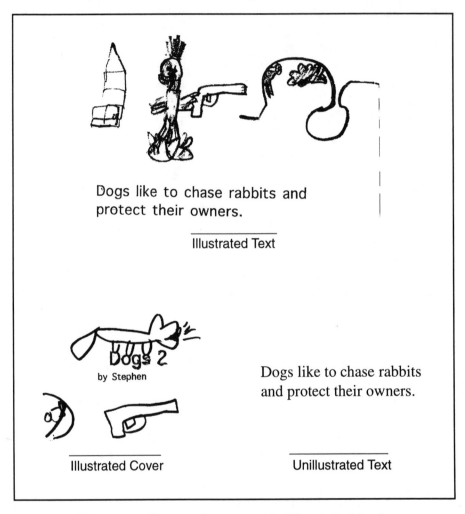

Figure 1.5   Illustrated cover and text for student book.

Whether or not a child has been in an organized preschool program, kindergartners have never been in an environment like an elementary school before. Incoming kindergartners *and their parents* are fragile and need to be treated gently. It is essential to follow John Dewey's advice and "start where the child is." It is important to establish a positive relationship with even the most difficult of children. Once rapport is established, children can and do accept constructive comments and build on them over time. It is easy to get discouraged at the slow pace of progress for some children. Keeping anecdotal records or taking occasional rate charts to measure progress in a problem area has helped me recognize and celebrate with them the small victories they achieve. Accessing and dealing with all the children's behaviors early in the year, while difficult, is essential. For me the key is in accepting each child as both important and as an individual. Reflecting on what they are trying to show me and what I can do to help them be successful is my constant focus.

Thinking through procedures ahead of time and making exact expectations clear to the children result in a classroom that usually runs smoothly—a classroom where children learn. Patience and repetition are the pivot points for turning the occasional chaos of September into the orderly classroom of November where real, in-depth learning occurs. Reminding students of procedures they are to follow before beginning an activity and helping them evaluate how well an activity went are good tools. What seems like a major investment of time spent helping students learn procedures early in the year eventually yields children who are in charge, who are secure and independent, freeing me to work with individuals and small groups as the rest of the classroom runs in an orderly and organized fashion.

By the end of the year, children come to school expecting to learn. They are willing to take risks because they know they will be supported. They attempt tasks which are difficult because they expect to be successful, or are willing to ask for help if they need it. They are anxious to share their growing knowledge about the world with me and their classmates because they now know that we value what they have to say. Watching all that successful growth and bursting enthusiasm for learning is a joy. Only the students and I know how hard won it sometimes is.

At the end of each school year, I ask the children how they think they learned to read and write so well. As I conduct this informal survey, I also ask them who taught them. Most credit their parents, grandparents, and older siblings with teaching them about letters and words and things of that sort. Few, if any, children are aware of the teaching that has gone on in the classroom. One year, a little boy looked at me with concern and said, "Ms. Edwards, we didn't learn, it's just what we do all day." I am especially proud of that response because in many ways it is absolutely true. I am proud of my own invisibility in their learning process. The fact that such powerful learning takes place so easily and naturally tells me we must be doing many things right. But the quintessential confirmation came recently from one little girl who, when asked how she and her classmates had learned to read and write so well, said, "You know, Mrs. Edwards, we just taught ourselves!"

References

Cambourne, B. (1988). *The whole story: Natural learning and the acquisition of literacy in the classroom.* Auckland, New Zealand: Ashton-Scholastic.

Edwards, L. (1994). Kidseye view of reading: Kindergartners talk about learning to read. *Childhood Education.* 70:3, 137-141.

Horner, J., & Gorman, J. (1985). *Maia: A dinosaur grows up.* Philadelphia, PA: Running Press.

Paley, (1981). *Wally's stories.* Cambridge, MA: Harvard University Press.

Chapter 2

Being Loved by Thank Yous!: Rural First Graders Make Connections

Tina DeStephen

Crystal, Ruth, and Dickey are three children who are among my most undeniable success stories. *Crystal* will soon be in high school. I don't see her very often now, but I hear how well she is doing. She used to come by my room and drop off notes telling me how much I had helped her, how I was *"like her mother, but not her mother."* Although she came from a loving family, Crystal's parents were poor and unable to provide the many educational resources and opportunities she needed. Yet Crystal truly wanted to learn and, with the chance to take control of her own learning during the two years she spent in my classroom, she did just that.

Crystal came to me as a cheerful six-year-old. Like others in the class, she was placed in the transitional program "pre-first", between kindergarten and first grade, because she didn't know all her "skills", and she was "immature". Some students were sent to pre-first because they had trouble socializing, but not Crystal. On the contrary, she was always friendly and talkative, and I realized from the beginning that verbal ability would be her pathway into literacy. In reviewing Crystal's progress that first year, I saw how far she had come, how many small successes had led to the growth I saw by April and May of that first year. Crystal was a success in our classroom, and she will be a lifelong learner, because of the attitudes toward learning she developed during that initial year.

In August of her pre-first year, I wrote about Crystal: [She] "wants to please, helpful, tries to answer for others and do all jobs, extremely verbal, tells wonderful oral stories from pictures." By mid-September I noted: "Works independently; needs help completing tasks. Is trying squiggly lines for writing in her journal; she is at the picture labeling stage." By the first part of December I observed that Crystal was: "Comfortable with copying from environment. Uses friends as experts for spelling words. Mirror writing. Better initial consonants: wrote *Rainbow Book* and distinguished between "sun" and "rainbow" with initial consonants."

Sometime during February I recorded that *"Crystal writes quickly. Now uses one letter per word, has some letter/sound correspondence! Uses fewer letters. " OUBIF"* : (Will you be my friend?) She is excited about writing." In the April/May entries, Crystal was observed: "Reading song charts; points and self-corrects when skips words. Substitutes synonyms for words she doesn't know. Good finger pointing/word correspondence. Remembers patterns well in stories."

On the last day of school that first year, I had a writing conference with Crystal. I was amazed to note five major writing breakthroughs at once: "Capitals at the beginning of sentences, end marks, spaces between all words, conventional spellings from the classroom environment, and final letter-sound correspondences." Crystal never got as frustrated as I did. She had obviously been sorting all these elements out in her mind for some time. She energetically began each session determined to do the best she could as she figured out what was going on that day. She showed me how personal the process of learning is and how every student must, in the end, find her own way.

My notes demonstrate how Crystal was coming to literacy in her own style and in her own time. Watching Crystal was fascinating. As she struggled to involve letter/sound correspondence in her reading and writing, she overcompensated at first. Sometimes she wrote *too many* letters for her words, causing her to sweep her finger over long strings of letters while reading only a few words. Other times she wrote *too few* letters. She used both styles within the same piece of writing. It was all part of her evolution into understanding the graphophonic system.

I especially didn't want to let Crystal go for the summer or to another classroom in the fall. She was blossoming right before my eyes in the last minutes of that school year. Crystal and four other of my pre-first students were placed in my first grade the next year. Sometimes you just get lucky!

These veterans of one year in my classroom became the helpers and leaders in first grade. They were excited about learning. They viewed themselves as competent people, and they immediately informed me of their needs and urged me to get things going quickly. "When will we start publishing?" "Why isn't the easel up yet?" "Can we get out the instruments now? I want to make up a song." "Can we do plays on our own soon?"

They were eager to make their own choices and set up some of their own agendas for learning. I wanted to observe the continued growth of these children. I was especially interested in working with Crystal.

Crystal turned out to be the obvious leader in the new classroom. She was in charge of her own learning and sometimes, everyone else's as well. That year was a constant search for balance between providing the original group continued experiences, yet not letting them overshadow the new kids. I encouraged Crystal and the other second year students to become mentors to the new children. As a result, they all grew and developed academically and in terms of self-confidence.

In September of the second year I wrote, "Crystal uses context and graphic cues. Seems tuned in to letters and sounds; wordness is really getting there. Writing has progressed since June (without my help!) Literacy is beginning to come together."

By November I saw that, "She quickly finds conventional spellings in environment and uses them. Uses spaces. She is writing periods and using some capitals." In reading I noted, "She has trouble with prepositions. Trouble staying on one word. Reads to self, then to me fluently with expression. If there is a pattern she catches it quickly."

In the early spring, I observed her, "Trying quotation marks in her journal": MY CiZN SaD 'I' 'Wot' 'a' 'haM' 'BiGrt'.. SaD ShaNhNN. (My cousin said, "I want a hamburger," said Shannon.) She also wrote a note to the cleaning people telling them to not open the egg incubator, "DO NOT Petk the Top Up Ples (Do not pick the top up please).

Crystal had developed a clear understanding of the reading/writing processes. Her log indicates that she proudly read 39 small books the first year and 114 during her second year in my room, in addition to the many library books, big books, children's published books, and various other books shared with the children. She thoroughly accessed all the resources in our classroom environment to help her grow as an independent learner.

Her sense of audience in her writing had been apparent throughout. She was totally involved in the social nature of literacy. She wrote numerous notes to other children in class and was a faithful pen-pal correspondent to a fifth grade student in our school. She used literacy to serve her own purposes and to solve problems that would benefit her classmates, such as this note of complaint:

("*Every time when the girls go in the bathroom in our room, we put (the sign) "Somebody is in the bathroom." Then the boys come in when we got it on. Crystal.*)

Figure 2.1 Crystal's note

Crystal tried many strategies to help her make sense of literacy. Her thinking was scattered at first, but that didn't stop her from writing. One story included several separate ideas: how nice I was; what she did when she got home; the people she liked; and how she and her Mama watched "Days of Our Lives" on TV. Her first published book, *The Rainbow*, also illustrates this multiplicity of themes and issues for Crystal.

> **The Rainbow**
> *This strawberry is gonna touch the rainbow.*
> *The strawberry touch the sun.*
> *I'm glad the rainbow come back up in the sky.*
> *The apples touch the sun and she come back up in the sky.*
> *I do like the sun.*
> *I do like the rainbow.*
> *The end of the story.*

No one, neither her peers nor I, seemed to be able to help Crystal clarify her ideas. In peer conferences, when she asked other children if they understood the strawberry story, they said "No." However, they said they liked it anyway. It was published as it was written, and everyone read it. I think the children liked it because it was poetic.

In May of the second year, I used one of Crystal's stories to assess her understanding of book features, spelling, punctuation, and handwriting. It showed the tremendous progress she had made in learning and clarifying her thoughts. She had a clear understanding of the purposes of writing a book. She retained her personality as a copious writer, unable to resist the urge to socialize with her reading audience.

A Real Story.

Published by We Like to Write Press.

This summer.

Mrs. Sullivan comed over my home. She ask my mother, can me and Sabrina go to the Girl Scouts? My mom said, " I got to think about it," she said. Then she thought about it and she said , Yes we can go. "We have to go when school is out?" "Yes," said mother. I think it's going to be fun and funny. I do not know that they are going to serve food at the Girl Scouts. I hope so. I think Mrs. Sullivan is going to pick us up in her car. Do you know where we are going? We are going to the Girl Scouts. I am going to wear shorts to Girl Scouts and sometimes pants at the Girl Scouts. Have anybody have been to Girl Scouts? I like to know because I'm going there. After school is out. I haven't been there yet. I do not know what it loks like. Girls only goes to the Scouts. The boys goes to another one. Girls and Boys goes to different Scouts.
The End.

Crystal came from a background concerned primarily with economic survival. There were few materials for reading, writing, and exploring the world beyond her over-crowded household. However, her family enveloped her with love, and she was encouraged to do well in school. Our classroom provided the solid foundation she needed to begin her intellectual journey. This year, Crystal will graduate from high school with honors.

I started my own teaching journey in California in the late 1960s. I used everything I had been "trained" to do such as project-oriented, integrated units in social studies and science, open-ended questions, sensory experiences, and math manipulatives. I encouraged "creative writing" and assigned standard weekly spelling lists. I used Language Experience as we wrote our class "Daily News". I read aloud to children everyday. We scaffolded and spiraled and inquired. Those were the days when California led the nation in per pupil expenditures and in school achievement. That was the good news.

The bad news was that I also taught reading in homogeneous reading groups and used the basal in round-robin oral reading. I used skill sheets and workbooks, focusing children's attention on memorizing words, practicing isolated phonics in a hierarchy of skills, and centering the curriculum entirely on what the state and my school district said the children *should* learn to get them ready for the next grade. I assessed them to find out what their "weaknesses" were. The textbooks were the source of the curriculum, and I judged how well they learned on the basis of tests. The children did fairly well but were not outstanding, and they didn't seem to really love learning or even reading. It seemed to me that school should be better. I wanted to be one of those teachers who do amazing things with their students and who the students never forget.

I taught for three years gradually coming to realize that teaching was not what I had expected and I was not the teacher I wanted to be. I was overwhelmed by the steady stream of paperwork. My students paraded in and out of my room throughout the day for various pull-out programs. We were almost never together as a group. There were constant interruptions and a lack of continuity, but more important, there was no sense of cohesion in my classroom. My students and I had become lost in a maze of programs, policies, and statistics. I left teaching to begin my family, intending never to return to the bureaucratic morass of the public school classroom.

Fourteen years and four children later, our family moved to Albuquerque, New Mexico. Reluctant to teach again, I decided to give substitute teaching a short-term trial. I knew immediately how much I had missed working with young children; so when I was offered a full-time position in a third grade classroom, I took it. Of course, I taught the way I always had. My reading groups, in particular, were running smoothly. However, two students had me baffled. They could quote phonic and structural analysis rules. They could even identify words on cards some of the time, but they could not consistently remember them. More importantly, they had great difficulty retelling stories or answering comprehension questions. I was doing everything I had been "trained" to do, and yet these students were not succeeding. My old uneasiness returned. What was wrong? Is this as good as it gets?

Two university classes I took to become certified in New Mexico proved to be the catalyst that changed me forever as a teacher. Both were classes in diagnostic reading. One was a seminar focused on brain theory and what research shows about the functions of the chief organ involved in learning. The other course centered on specific tools for literacy assessment and evaluation. I learned to use assessments that were totally new to me: *Concepts About Print*, "Running Record", "Miscue Analysis", cloze procedures, reading and writing interviews, holistic scoring and other tools. I discovered new ways to teach and evaluate reading, writing, and spelling. I looked at story structure and the language children use, reading articles by well-known researchers and educators from the United States, England, Australia, and New Zealand. I became aware of the writing process and of reading as a matrix of connected strategies rather than a series of discrete skills operations.

Of course, I had to reexamine my teaching practices. I questioned the value of using sight word flash cards and isolated letter-sound drills from workbooks. I thought about the controlled language of the old basal readers, whose stories were really such bad literature. I reconsidered arbitrary spelling lists and grammar worksheets, and I discarded every practice that did not help emerging readers and writers make meaningful connections toward independence. As I explored new ways of teaching I found that I was loving learning and teaching again. I was enthralled with the progress my students made. Then, my husband was transfered, and we moved.

We left Albuquerque and the clear, dry air of the Sandia Mountains for the lush, rolling hills and humidity of middle Tennessee. For the last twelve years, I have been teaching in a small rural school, 30 miles outside of Nashville. Although I do not live in this tiny community, the smallness of the school and the close-knit quality of the surrounding area allow me the opportunity to know my students and their families quite well. Through home visits and local field trips, I am now well-acquainted with the many tobacco farms, dairies, horse farms, vegetable and fruit farms that dot the hillsides and flat fields in this area. I have seen, and smelled, the local battery recycling plant. My students and I have visited the post office, bank, small grocery store, drug store, gas station, flower store, grist mill, dairy supply store, and senior citizens center that are all situated along the main road running through the unincorporated village in which the school is located.

There is no bookstore or library in this community. Numerous small churches sprinkle the area. The majority of my students, however, do not attend church on a regular basis. The local baseball field is an important community site. Students are active in sports and receive enthusiastic parental and community support. Many children like to race with the train as it passes by on the one line of tracks going through the area. The most they can hope for is a whistle greeting. There is no longer a train station here.

My students would be classified as being from poor to lower middle class. Some of the families own their own houses. Many of them rent or live in trailers. Some have no tap water and must rely on water trucked in. Many of my students have their own bedrooms. Some of them share rooms with brothers and sisters, cousins, or even parents. Having grandparents nearby, even next-door, is not uncommon. Some homes have dogs and cats in the home; a few even have chickens living inside. All seem to have at least one TV and a VCR, bringing into their lives many influences the narrow, winding roads had formerly been able to forestall. Most homes have some books, especially the Bible, but only a few subscribe to a daily newspaper.

Although no one would expect these children to be well-acquainted with the more sophisticated life of Nashville, I assumed they would be steeped in knowledge that rural, farm life usually provides. Instead I found that the background knowledge the children held involved mostly what goes on inside their immediate households. Many children live on farms that are no longer productive. There are no herds of livestock to feed and watch, no crops to plant or harvest. The children watch TV as a major source of recreation rather than working and playing outdoors. They see the community from a distance, often coming no closer to it than the school bus window. It became apparent to me after a year in this area that the school environment needed to provide a great many direct experiences so that learning made sense and these children could connect with the wider world. The curriculum also needed to provide some of the many experiences absent from the children's lives and awareness.

In a learner-centered classroom the focus is on the needs and interests of the children. There are a variety of comfortable seating options: the rug, the floor, a beanbag, and chairs. There are numerous shelves for books and math and science materials, all within easy reach by the children. There is a large Discovery Table containing science materials for observation and exploration. There is one computer, as well as a typewriter and a listening center. Maps and globes are at child level for ease of access. A storytime rocker sits on a large rug near a chalkboard. We use it for group sharing and Author's Celebration when the children take "center stage" to share their published books. Several big book stands hold books for shared reading and for the students to use as they become the teacher of other students. The physical environment is supportive of interactive/collaborative learning.

The tables are grouped together to encourage oral language and the exchange of ideas for writing and collaborative projects. Tables and bookcases are clustered to form discrete areas, allowing children to sit beneath them and between them as they plan, read to each other, use math manipulatives and blocks, or play instruments and games. These physical groupings encourage the students to become independent learners, to turn to each other for assistance, and help each other when they can.

Because I want to foster a community environment in which everyone shares everything from ideas to materials, most materials are within easy reach by the children. There are shared materials in the Writing Center including a variety of papers, dictionaries, writing folders, pencils and markers, and colored editing pens and pencils. The Art Center contains construction and other papers, glue, scissors, a stapler, a hole punch, paper clips, drawing books, and stencils. All desk clusters contain a "school box" of crayons, and containers for pencils, colored markers, glue sticks, large erasers, and clear tape. The Discovery Center includes rulers, tape measures, scales, measuring cups, magnifying lenses, magnets and microscopes, all of which invite children to engage in math and science literacy. Both story and information books are placed throughout the room, as well as on the big books stand for the entire class. Other print resources include poetry, book sets for author and illustrator studies, text sets for themes under study, multiple copies of books for heterogeneous groups at Literature Study, magazines and catalogs, a telephone directory, maps, and an atlas.

The print-rich environment of our classroom evolves throughout the year. The boards, walls, and clotheslines become increasingly full of children's edited work and other visuals from our various learning expeditions. The children can find demonstrations of how print works through using the many charts, wall displays, sign-up forms, and clothesline hangings in the room. There are the typical ABC charts and handwriting forms, but in addition, our room displays a word wall with many word lists containing basic word patterns, sight words, and words that relate to the current themes and concepts under investigation. The children refer to all these resources as they read, write, and edit their writing. They also use personal writing dictionaries in which they look up commonly used words and add new words from their writing. They list about five words a week from their writing onto their "spelling rings" (cards attached to curtain rings) and use these for personal spelling "lists." We also make large books of "Language Collections": homophones, homographs, similes, etc., adding to these lists as we come across them.

There are shared writing charts with ideas generated by the students. The shared writings include: "Class Rules", a web of "What We Want to Learn" during the year, "Color Words" at the art center, "Number Words" near the math center, maps and globes with labels that are often used in writing, and an on-going time-line as we study historical events. We have webs and charts of different themes that show *What We Know, What We Want to Know, and What We Have Learned*. Themes being studied are represented through pictures and writing. The children demonstrate their growing literacy as they write in their journals or make labels for the science Discovery Table.

Emphasizing the many functions of language for organization and learning in our room, we employ forms and charts for: "Class Helpers", "Class Schedule", "The Publishing Process", a "Language Workshop List of Choices" (lasting two hours or more each day), as well as individual charts for the children to log observations and record what they do. A small flip sign tells them if I'm in a conference and not to be disturbed. There are many lists to read and write on: sign-ups for teacher conference, computer time, typewriter time, "Books I Want to Hear at Storytime", "Shared Book Time", "Author's Chair" time, and so on. There are student names to read that tell who is next to do the Attendance Tally for the week, who will illustrate the Class News for the day and copy it into our weekly newspaper, who is to lead Morning Routines, and who paints at the easel next. In short, the children are immersed in literacy and content, the many functions of written language, and the responsibilities or managing or otherwise participating in a classroom community of learners.

As their teacher, I intentionally demonstrate the functions and surface features of written language as we do Guided Reading and Shared Writing in groups and prepare the Class News. I show them patterns, and we share our observations about phonics, punctuation, capitalization, spelling, and grammar, even different functions and genres of writing. We discuss words on song charts, in Big Books, in writing we come across in books, and writing seen throughout the room, school and community. I continually urge my students to become keen observers of their environments. They, in their own time, become the leaders, informing me about what they notice and making connections between what we learn in the classroom and life in the wider world beyond.

In the beginning, I act sometimes as their secretary, recording for them until they can record for themselves. For instance, as we recorded the events and sensory experiences during our trip to the local fruit and vegetable stand, the children became interested in the function that "silent e" plays at the end of words indicating the long sound of the preceding vowel. The children wanted me to help them list some of the spelling generalizations and related examples we noticed. I did so and then we hung the list on the wall for everyone to see and use. The "rules" we list remind the children what to do as they read and write. The rules for writing and spelling are *usually,* but not always, consistent. The students are encouraged to apply all these rules and demonstrations as they read, write stories and correspondence, or in their journals, logs, and notebooks.

I overtly demonstrate learning in other ways as well. I demonstrate how I learn, in effect thinking out-loud. I ask questions and show the reasoning I use to solve problems, and I encourage them to do the same. This year, we had a mural of dinosaurs painted in our cafeteria by local artists. After visiting the science museum, observing sea animal fossils from the area, and learning that Tennessee had at one time been under water, I helped the children reflect back to the mural. We answered questions like, "Do you think the lake in the mural was part of the water that covered the land in Tennessee? Do you know what I just thought about? Was middle Tennessee covered by water before or after the dinosaurs? Why do you think so? Where could we go to find out? Who could we ask who might know?"

This was not an invented scenario for the purpose of following a lesson plan on using resources to answer questions. These were authentic questions that developed on the spot as the children and I discussed and reflected upon our shared field trip experience. I want my children to see the importance of asking questions and knowing how to find the answers. With those tools and values in hand, they can each continue to grow as lifelong learners. The students are supported as individual learners as they make connections between what they already know, what we are learning, and what they want to know more about. They are encouraged at every possible opportunity, in writing and group discussions, to make personal responses to what they are encountering.

Response, a key part of Storytime as well as Quiet Self-Selected Reading (QSSR), confirms the importance of their own thinking, ideas, and interests. When I read stories or poems to my students, I elicit their responses by asking, "What did you like about the story?" "What did it remind you about in your own life?" "What other books (programs, authors, illustrators, etc.), did this remind you of?" Hearing what others say helps us enlarge our own connections. It also helps us accept the connections that others make because of their different background knowledge, experiences, and values.

When children write in their response logs after silent reading time, they are asked to respond to what they read that day. They know that as they read they are to think about what it means to them. As my students read to me in reading conference, I encourage them to do more than read word by word. For example, when I asked Michael how he corrected something he read, he replied, "I thinked in my head and I went back."

As children begin to make their own successful corrections, I overhear remarks like "Don't help me. I'm gonna guess it." As they make appropriate substitutions and leave out or insert words to make the language make sense, I realize that they are responding to and constructing meaning for themselves. As we reread and work out the hard words, I realize how much they are learning about phonic patterns, what written language is, and how it works. I see them making reading and writing their own.

I wish all parents could see their children and their language and learning the way I do. When Matt wrote: *"It is fun to write. When you write, it feels like you are drawing YOU!"*, I thought, children can be as naturally profound as adults. They are philosophers and poets, and their parents don't usually get to appreciate those events. After receiving several thank you notes in his mailbox, James wrote to me:

"I loved being loved by Thank You's"

There is never a question in my classroom that we are there for serious learning. Even though we maintain an atmosphere of informality, I expect them to do their best, and they know it. One year, Terry's family began building a new house. His continued questions and sharings generated a theme on houses: the construction of houses, animal houses, and people's houses. This expanded until we were learning about houses throughout the world. We explored tools. We took field trips to see barns being built. We visited an exhibit of artistically created gingerbread houses. At the beginning of the year, I had no thought of studying houses and neither did the children. Terry's overwhelming curiosity and desire propelled us throughout this study. The children did the work. They wrote, read, questioned, acted out their story ideas, pretended to be builders, and in the process learned a wealth of information, math skills, vocabulary and concepts. Children at risk become vitalized as they see what they can do and what they have learned.

Our themes involve every possible curricular area that is appropriate and meaningful. Children are included in decisions about planning each theme, researching it, and sharing their information. They are part of the process of delving deeper, expanding one theme into another as a natural evolution from the previous topic area or beginning a new theme that has emerged from an event in the community or our classroom. One year, after seeing the play "Jack and the Beanstalk," we read many different versions of the story. This led us to a comparison of "giant" stories and tall tales, particularly those of Steven Kellogg. We drew webs of what we knew about giants. The children then became interested in studying dinosaurs, followed by whales. The children's interest in and discussions of giant things eventually led to an interest in "little people." We were in the midst of enjoying fairy stories when we ran out of time at the end of the year. That theme cycle ran from November until June, with other theme areas interspersed. Their interest continued into the next school year! So much for children's reported short attention spans.

As the teacher, I want to facilitate learning rather than be the only "expert." Although I teach directly every day in reading, writing, math, spelling, phonics, and more, I also encourage students help each other. Together they learn to share, plan, problem solve, and extend their learning and their knowledge of available resources. It is evident that Rayann regarded me as just one of many available teachers when she wrote for the Message Board: "I love this class because they help me learn, Mrs. De Stephen too, and help me learn my name.

Figure 2.2 Rayann's message

My students are both teachers and learners in their own classroom, and that has a dramatic effect on everyone. The first year I was in Tennessee I had a four year age span in my room. In addition to kindergarten and pre-first students, there were two children repeating first grade, both of whom were obviously at risk.

Eight-year-old *Ruth* was unhappy about repeating first grade. Ruth made astounding progress during that year, despite a high number of absences and very little in the way of "standard" literacy at home. I was told that I had taught her to read when nothing else had. I prefer to think that Ruth connected with a philosophy of learning that valued her as a learner and that placed her in the center of meaningful, interactive language and learning events. She began the class shy and insecure, afraid to take risks, reluctant to share what she knew, and doing the minimum amount of work necessary. Her first "blank book" in September read:

by Ruth _____
The lion was going to sleep.
The rainbow came out.
The rainbow came out.
The End of Ruth's book

As the year progressed, Ruth began to understand that she knew a great deal which she could use to help herself and the other children learn. The more she shared, the more she grew in her own understandings in all areas of the curriculum. She began to use her time well, to take children aside and help them, to use her own writing for a variety of purposes, and to share in large group with confidence. In the spring she spent several weeks writing and publishing a story, sharing a special time in her life. The following story, and the process Ruth went through in taking charge of her own learning, provide eloquent evidence of the success she achieved and the promise she felt. Written in the spring of that year, and progressing through several drafts, it demonstrates how far she had come.

My Granny's Pony Died

by Ruth

When it was a snowy day, my Mama, my Granny, Hollis, and me had to go out in the woods. We had to find my Granny's pony. Friday the 13th my Granny's pony died. Me and my Granny cried.

We buried him beside the creek where he did die. They tied the string around one foot. Then they tied the string around the pole.

They pulled him in the hole that they dig for him. Then they put the dirt over him.

Me and my cousins put some buttercups on his grave. My Granny and my Mama put a fence around his grave. My Granny put some flowers on his grave. When they will grow, they will grow all over his grave.

He was 17. We was very sad. He was the greatest pony in the whole world. I loved him very, very much. And my Granny, she loved him too. He is still my Granny's pony.

That year was a turning point for Ruth. She had changed her attitude about herself from school failure to valuable contributing member of a learning community. She is on the path toward lifelong learning. Like Crystal, Ruth is also a successful high school student today. I have watched both girls and numerous other children become good students and self-directed learners. I often wonder what would have happened to them if they had started in a more rigid, mechanistic program? Their voices ring in my ears. I can still hear their questions and the wonderful ideas they had. The effect of such empowerment can also be seen in Dickey's development across the two years he was in my classroom.

Dickey came to me as an easily distractible 6-1/2 year old. He often arrived at school hungry. I learned to keep peanut butter and crackers on hand just for him. It was difficult for the family to bring water into the home, so I often encouraged him to wash up at school. He was aware of the reactions of others toward him and showed marked insecurity. I wanted to help him value himself as a person. I hoped I could get the rest of the class to value his ideas and abilities as well. Dickey's success was remarkable.

Over the course of his pre-first and first grade years he went from a boy most of the other children avoided to one of the class favorites. He developed a reputation as creative, as an innovative thinker. Everyone came to know him as quick to size up problems and find practical solutions. He was able to apply math in everyday situations. He also became our chief carpenter and handyman.

In the autumn of the first year, Dickey drew pictures in blank books as his journal. For him, the story "was in the picture". When he read his own writing or other books, he "read" the picture alone. He experimented with squiggly lines for writing. Although he had good phonic knowledge, at first he didn't relate it to print. As the year progressed, he started to reread his own stories and write more. He loved to sing his favorite song, *Turkey in the Straw*. His voice rang with gusto, "Turkey and a frog, Ha, Ha, Ha." During Shared Reading of song charts, Dickey began to focus on sound/letter correspondences. It was group singing that first hooked him on written literacy. His journals and other writing then began to reflect accurate initial consonant letter/sound correspondences.

By winter, Dickey was using more than one consonant per word: "*Tte*" (today). He began to use conventional spelling from around the room. He became aware of the social nature of writing. He wrote a class note on the broken typewriter: "NOBETN" (Nobody typing) to let everyone know that nobody would be able to type. Without asking, he took over the job of writing the date on the chalkboard. As he developed, his writing became fast and messy; his reading even faster and messier. During conferences he would silently read ahead before reading the same part of the text out loud to me. But he definitely focused on meaning.

I tried to help Dickey understand that we write for people to read our thoughts, and therefore smaller, more legible writing with spaces between words is important. He was learning initial and final sounds as well as beginning to insert vowel letters in some words. By January his contribution in the small-group, collaborative newspaper read: "I BD A BFOD AD HE TS" (I bought a billfold at Harry Taylor's [grocery]). He was reading back his own writing easily. Next, he actually read Bill Martin's *Brown Bear, Brown Bear, What Do You See?* without using the pictures, thinking it through for meaning, remembering part of the pattern, and using graphophonic clues.

By spring of that first year, he was writing about many things important in his life: his father's "spell" (illness), a race he had with another child, and driving the family truck. His stories became longer, and his illustrations supported the writing rather than the other way around. He was using spacing, and his writing had become somewhat smaller and neater. He began to use more complex sentence structure: "When I get home, I will drive my car down the road." His spelling was improving. Dickey was on his way.

His reading also showed marked progress. He read more difficult books. He was persistent and successful. He was using all three language cue systems, the semantic, syntactic, and graphophonic. He knew if something didn't "fit", even though he was not always sure what to do about it. He remembered what he'd already read. He would look back to find words he had previously seen in a story and use them in new passages. He was developing good sight vocabulary. His attention span increased considerably, and he was happy.

By the end of that year, Dickey was intensely interested in writing and could concentrate for long periods of time. His ideas were wonderful and his language ever more expressive. He was patient, sometimes working on reading and rereading a book for two or more days. He used good prediction, confirmation, and correction strategies when he read. His Mom told me, "I don't know what ya done to him, but he don't want to miss no school. He'd come to school even if he was 'dyin'."

Dickey, like Crystal, went to first grade in my classroom the next year. As a proficient member of a meaning-centered classroom using functional experiences and hands-on projects, he grew tremendously and served as a mentor to the new students. Through fall, Dickey wrote longer stories, sometimes all in one sentence, but then he began revising his stories. With one story he wrote the middle first, added the end, and then wrote the beginning to tell where the story took place. He decided that his story needed those revisions, reordering the sections during Language Workshop. He would often work intensely on his writing, revising and editing for the entire block of time. "When I get to coloring and writing, I can't stop." he volunteered one day.

The following March entry from Dickey's first grade year shows the humor and expressive quality of his writing.

> *The Car*
> *I seen a car.*
> *Riding down the road.*
> *It stopped. I said, "Where is that car stopping?"*
> *I follered it on my bike.*
> *It stopped at my house.*
> *I said, "What's up Doc?"*
> *It was David. We played. The End*

Dickey took for himself the freedom to create with language. Following an author's study on Robert Munsch, the class sent Munsch several letters. In response, he sent us an autographed picture, signed "Bob Munsch". In his autograph, he played with the letters in his name by drawing himself bearded in place of the "o" in "Bob." Dickey immediately incorporated this playfulness into his own writing by drawing a bearded man in place of some of his vowels as he wrote: *"When me and my brother was playing kickball, my ball busted."*

Figure 2.3 Dickey's Writing

By the end of that second year, Dickey was reading and writing like most any other first grader. He felt comfortable sharing his ideas with the class and leading us into new experiences. He sang songs from the song chart with great joy. He suggested we act out songs and stories. He related to and participated willingly in science and social studies projects. He talked about the information and concepts he was learning. In the end, he was ready for second grade.

Each class I have includes many children like Crystal, Ruth and Dickey. They have unique personalities, varied interests and strengths. While schools cannot solve all of their complex problems, these children are vulnerable. They are easily hurt and more easily lost. Their growth into life-long learning depends on how soon, and how well they experience acceptance and success, find their own voices, ask their own questions, and connect with their own understandings.

These children helped me learn how to teach them. And I have discovered that only when I reflectively keep the children themselves at the heart of the process, am I doing my job. I help them make the world make sense, relate their past understandings to new knowledge, accept and respect their language and culture, ensure that they experience success in my classroom, protect them from themselves and others, and teach them to care by treating them with care. Only then can they overcome the considerations which put them at risk of school failure in the first place.

References

Butler, A., & Turbill, J. (1985). *Towards a reading-writing classroom*. Portsmouth, NH: Heinemann.

Cambourne, B. & Turbill, J. (1988). *Coping with chaos*. Portsmouth, NH: Heinemann.

Hansen, J. (1987). *When writers read*. Portsmouth, NH: Heinemann.

Martin, B. (1967). *Brown bear, brown bear. What do you see?* New York, NY: Holt, Hinehart and Winston.

Chapter 3

"I Can Read So Good 'Cause I Write So Much": Learning From and With Inner-City Second Graders

Melanie Ricks

We live in a highly literate society where the ability to read and write is an absolute necessity. Minimal literacy is just no longer good enough, especially for the demands of the 21st century. Being able to decode without being able to understand is not even minimal, nor does it allow young people who are at risk to move out of poverty. In advanced technological democracies, reading requires more than identifying words, and writing requires more than barely being able to fill out a job application at a fast food restaurant.

It is through reading, through good narratives and high quality non-fiction that children acquire new ideas, making the necessary cognitive connections that allow them to learn and grow in skill and confidence. Experiences with good books allow us to explore our diversity as members of various cultural groups, our uniqueness as individuals, and the common bonds that unite us all as human beings. There is more to reading and writing than the mastery of surface features, the mechanics of print, and the mere recognition of basic words. Full literacy requires that learners have in-depth, personal experiences with a wide variety of concepts through good literature and other print sources (Short

& Burke, 1992). What constitutes the literacy needs of all citizens in our society? What kinds of classrooms best produce students who will understand and value democratic ideals? What instructional experiences create successful, independent learners, children who like to learn and who can use information to synthesize, generalize, and apply conclusions critically for solving problems? What can teachers do to ensure high levels of literacy for the various groups of learners, especially children of the urban poor? These are some of the issues and questions that occupied my mind and furthered my thinking as I began teaching second grade in an inner-city elementary school.

THE SCHOOL

My school houses 450 children, grades K-4, accommodating most of them in portable classrooms both in front of, and behind, the main structure. Eighteen classrooms are outside while only 10 are inside the original main building. Located at the edge of a large federally subsidized housing project, the school serves the project and surrounding homes in a two mile radius. The school's racial mix is 60% black, 35% white and 5% newly immigrated Asian children. More than 80% of the children benefit from the free lunch program. The portable classrooms testify to the rapid growth of this neighborhood, as more and more families have had to move to low income housing. These are children of poverty. Most live in single parent households or in situations without either parent. A substantial number of young people from this area never finish high school, and many end up in prison or worse.

The neighborhood is in an area of the city plagued by violent crime and high unemployment. From behind the playground in back of the school, which the children are no longer allowed to use, daily drug deals, car thefts, and occasional murders take place. Though the school only includes kindergarten through fourth grade, some of its children already have sexually transmitted diseases, are otherwise abused or neglected, or suffer from other traumas that young children should never have to face. Some of the children in this school have themselves been involved in violence, are already well acquainted with illegal drugs, and carry weapons whenever they can. They live in a war zone and they are habitually angry, frightened, and sad.

And yet, this school is a place where children are learning, where most of them want to be, and where parents have pride and a sense of belonging. Many teachers have collected extensive numbers of children's books for their classrooms. Often at their own expense, they have attended workshops and seminars around the country or enrolled in graduate classes on developmental literacy and language assessment. They have collected and read a wealth of professional literature and continue to search out information on the latest instructional techniques. Most of the teachers in this school are trying valiantly to support children's learning rather than trying to make the children fit within the old curriculum (Taylor, 1991).

THE CLASSROOM

The classroom in which I teach is a portable in front of the main building. It is a second grade where the children are engaged in reading and writing nearly all day, every day. With the exception of an hour each of direct instruction in reading and math, essentially everything is integrated into the current unit of study. The children work on themes they choose involving much additional individual choice and small group planning. When they aren't in one large group at the rug area being read to, the children typically scatter throughout the room working alone, in pairs or small groups. More than 1000 children's books are on display and in use at all times in my classroom. Often, my children are seen reading a book or working on a project during lunch or in other locations around the school, a rare sight in many inner-city schools.

In addition to good books, an abundance of other print sources are available. These include newspapers, magazines, catalogs, notes pinned to the message board, and items from the class grocery store. The children's writing, other projects, lists of various types, and captioned art work cover the walls, hang from clotheslines stretched across the ceiling, and are displayed on tables at the back of the room. Tables are arranged to provide extended work surfaces for the children and to facilitate the children's collaborative efforts. A listening center, a science experiment and observation area, a post office, and a computer center also occupy the room. The room, although colorful, has a well used and lived-in appearance. Children's "work in progress" is everywhere. This is very much a learner centered classroom.

Every morning, during book share, the children read or retell favorite stories. They read their own writing and discuss work in progress during group share and Author's Chair. They read and talk about good books focusing on how the characters, issues and events relate to other books they've read or to their own lives. They write everyday and bring information and objects of interest into the classroom for everyone to experience and write about. They view learning as making sense of the world around them. They help each other pursue topics and they help each other become independent and successful.

THE SCHEDULE

The schedule is always complicated with all the extra activities, special pull-out programs, and other classes like computer, not to mention interruptions from the office. This year, we have a two-hour and forty-five minute block of time in the morning. That's when we do math and reading/writing workshop. It is working out very well. The biggest problem is that we get into reading or writing, or into math, and we don't want to quit. The children solved this problem by suggesting that we flip-flop language workshop and math. One week it's math first, and the next week it's reading/writing. That way, if we short change the second subject, it will even out over time.

My instructional program was not always so learner-centered or literacy and content rich. Like many teachers, I was taught to follow the basal reader and other textbook manuals. I learned to group children by ability and to separate the school day into subjects, and the subjects, especially math and language arts, into isolated, decontextualized skills. When I first started teaching, I taught strictly from the books, drilling children on "skills", making them sit in rows, telling them not to talk to each other and requiring them always to do their own work.

I taught in the primary grades for 10 years using traditional methods. I tested, grouped, taught, retaught, and retested. Most of the children never moved out of the groups in which I initially placed them. The children did not excel, and many appeared to be completely uninterested in school even by second grade. I never saw children come to love learning. I never saw children who were able to make an inspired leap in growth that might alter the course of their lives. Eventually, I concluded this just isn't working! These are bright children, but they aren't learning as much or as readily as they could. The stories in the basal reader aren't very good, and the children are bored. If I hate reading the same kind of story in the same way week after week, I know the children do, too. I just knew there had to be a better way!

I always believed in and valued reading good books to the children. But I felt such pressure to follow the prescribed curriculum that I would put reading aloud last, reading only if I had time. But I decided I simply had to read aloud to the children everyday. They needed to hear the language of good books. I also knew I wanted them to write more. So that was the driving force for me. I began to pay closer attention to my students as individuals. What were they trying to show me about their learning? How could I teach them in ways that empowered them as independent learners and challenged them to do their best? How could I engage them in learning activities and create authentic experiences for them? How could I support their self evaluation and taking responsibility for their own learning?

PAST STUDENTS

Most of my students are seven, eight, and nine-year-olds. At those ages, children are highly curious. They are very aware of fairness issues. They are becoming concerned with what other kids think about them, and they also want to know about their immediate environment. In addition to all that, many of my students are aggressive and angry. But at the same time, they are usually anxious to please, especially their teachers. They need praise and encouragement. What that tells me as a teacher is that these children need great amounts of information, a safe environment in which to explore and express themselves, and genuine success. They don't have to succeed at everything they try; learning also takes place when we try and do not succeed. But they do have to experience success often enough to discover that they can do some things well. I want them to find out for themselves what genuine success feels like and to experience the fact that success breeds more success.

I knew that what I had been doing in following the textbooks, the curriculum guide, and the achievement test as the basis for my curriculum was simply not enough. It was actually robbing the children of what they needed most from school.

I was concerned about student learning, so the first thing I started was a classroom writing program modeled after Writers' Workshop, implementing the use of journals and story-starters because that was all I knew to do. And I allowed them time and opportunity to write. However, I was also concerned about their values. I believed these children had to be willing to take risks and work together if they were going to develop the potential I knew they had. So we implemented a positive approach to discipline, as well as a conflict resolution program. I read good books to the children, sometimes three or four a day, often reading each book more than once. That was nearly ten years ago. I kept the basals the first year and dispensed with the workbooks. I never did use many ditto sheets, so getting rid of them was not difficult.

The basal readers remained in the room the second year, but we only used them a few times. Now I have several that are more like anthologies of children's literature, and I use them as multiple copies of stories we read as we choose. I also involve more writing and classroom publishing with the children. We make shape books and a variety of other hard and soft cover books. I finally let go and encouraged the children to choose their own topics to write about if they wanted to. I learned about personal involvement in writing and what produces the best writing from my students. Now I *require* that they choose their own topics. And, I model writing in class for them to see—not only to let them see that I write and that I like to write, but how I go about it. I tried out new ideas and evaluated what was and what wasn't effective.

I was in the process of figuring out my own teaching philosophy. I listed belief statements that made sense to me. I wrote them down on cards and kept them at my desk: "Children learn language by using language in real ways." "We learn to read as we read to learn." "Start where the child is." "Language is the gift we use to make sense of our world."

I really relied on a statement from Brian Cambourne that people can't focus on the window and see the scene beyond at the same time. And, young children can't focus on meaning and the language being used to convey that meaning simultaneously. That one insight really helped me focus in on what I wanted to do and why. The gist was that I wanted to focus on meaning first.

Reminding myself that it is the process of learning that is important, not any one product, I encourage my students to organize and carry out very sophisticated activities and projects. I have to keep them challenged, and I have to provide enough support so they successfully grapple with in-depth issues and concepts. I encourage them to help each other and to find information on their own. I require that they ask their own questions—what they want to do or know about. I require that they ask important questions, and they come to know the difference between frivolous and significant questions and issues.

If I ask them questions, I ask "What do you think about this? How does this make you feel? What do you want to do next? How can I help you? How can we find that information? How can you go about answering your question?" I show them that resources are everywhere, that they learn from each other as well as from books, multiple print sources, the environment, and me.

At the first of each year, students aren't a community of learners yet. Sometimes a class achieves that sense of community by the third week, and sometimes it takes as long as two months. It requires time and intentional experiences to create a cooperative, inquiry-based classroom. As part of what I want the children to experience, we plan together: we discuss choices and options; we design our room; we take care of business; and we evaluate together.

Evaluation is one of the things I really work on. I want the children to see just how far they've come. They keep a portfolio with at least one piece of work to include every six weeks. They also keep writing and math learning logs and we reread them from time to time as a record of where they were and where they are now. Their logs have been among the most effective device I've used.

Taking care of business occurs primarily during morning routines and check-in time at the beginning of each day. Morning routines include taking the roll, checking the weather and the calendar, adding to our days in school number line, saying the pledge, singing songs and reading poems together. The children are in charge of these duties, and I am there to help if they need me. We also go over the newspaper from the day before. The class I have this year really loves sports figures, so we read about sports figures everyday. The children cut out the ones they like best. We also look for "peace makers" in the paper. Any article about someone who helps someone else is a peace maker article. The children keep a display of sports figures and a scrapbook on peace makers. Sometimes these articles provide wonderful fuel for intense class discussions and writing.

Every morning, I ask if there is anything people want to talk about or if there are any questions. During that time, I teach them as best I can how to take care of themselves. Most of the time, they want to tell about going someplace or getting something as a present. But sometimes they need to talk about something bad that has happened or about their fears: somebody died, there was a stabbing, a shooting, or a drug deal that went wrong. And we talk about how they feel. We also talk about what to do if you hear something that sounds like gunfire or if a stranger knocks on your door. When everyone has had a chance to "debrief", so to speak, and we are all feeling reassured, we sing a song, have a group hug, and then we are ready to begin our school day. I have learned that daily debriefing and a togetherness routine is necessary before the children can leave the street behind and get into a mindset for learning. Occasionally, we also get some really good writing from these morning routines (Peterson, 1995).

THIS YEAR'S GROUP

This year's group became a family of learners very quickly. Not only are the children making good choices and having wonderful ideas and questions, but they have really learned the conflict resolution format too. Yesterday, one of the bigger boys pushed one of the smaller girls because he thought she was cutting in front of him in line. They ended up slapping at each other. They weren't hurt, but both children were angry. I asked them if they wanted me to solve their problem by deciding what should happen or if they wanted to go to mediation. They both said they wanted mediation. So after school we met and *they* decided: a) they would ask rather than push, b) they would not use their hands and feet to solve their problems, and c) they wanted to be friends and to work it out. I also asked them to agree to remember these decisions.

We are starting our first theme study next week. The children are interested in how things change. One child brought in two toads and another child brought a frog. We have been reading Frog and Toad stories ever since. We've also been reading about the differences between toads and frogs. Then the children wanted to know about other life forms that go through metamorphosis. Some of them knew about butterflies. While we were talking about what we had found out about toads and frogs, someone else said everything changes, we all change, and that's how the idea got started. I can see lots of ways to make connections with what we have already been learning. We've been looking at patterns in numbers and patterns in nature. And I'm sure someone will connect how we change to the conflict resolution process. In fact, I think that is why they wanted to know about change because they already feel themselves changing.

Making connections and making sense of what we are studying for ourselves is at the heart of learning in my classroom, and the children are so good at it. I have also spent a lot of time and money to fill this classroom up with culturally relevant and culturally diverse literature. Some of the money was my own, but most came from grant monies. Last year, the children loved *The Black Snowman* by Mendez most. This year, already, they are wild about Climo's *The Egyptian Cinderella, An Enchanted Hair Tale* by DeVeaux, and *If You Give a Mouse A Cookie* by Numeroff. So we are going back to previously shared books like those and talking about changes we see in favorite texts.

When I first began trying to alter my teaching, I didn't really know if I was on the right track or not. However, I knew the children would tell me. I watched what they were doing, what they seemed to be learning, and how they were reacting. I tried to look beyond the surface to see if I could detect positive changes in abilities and attitudes. I first saw what I was looking for as I watched Angel, Lynn, and Gerald.

Angel was taller, older, and louder than any of the other children. She was almost a behavior problem in the beginning, then I realized much of her acting out in class was because she felt so awkward and out of place. She lived with her mother and younger brother. Her father was never mentioned. They were a very low income family. Angel was not only tall; she was one of the thinnest children I've ever seen. Often she wore clothes that were too small for her rapidly growing body. She sucked the middle two fingers of her left hand while she worked; her nose ran almost constantly during the fall and winter months; and she could barely read. Initially, I thought I wouldn't see much progress from Angel. I was afraid she was a slow learner. She had repeated one year already and had a transition year between kindergarten and first grade, making her two years behind her age group in school.

When she started second grade, she would only copy writing, and she wouldn't read anything at all. She copied simple books and other print in the room. I supposed she was teaching herself in a way that seemed safe and reasonable to her. Toward the end of September, something happened about which she was extremely excited, and she produced this piece of unsolicited text.

Figure 3.1 Angel's Thank-You Note

It was a spontaneous thank-you note to the kindergarten teacher who had provided our classroom with baby gerbils. Angel loved the baby gerbils, and had been moved to communicate with the giver. I saw how her writing resembled the writing of the emerging five or six-year-old. I noticed her use of consonants and her understanding of wordness and space. I was thrilled. I suggested that she take the note to Ms. Waddell. She was so proud of herself. That was a breakthrough for her. After the thank-you note about the gerbils and having teachers actually tell her she had done something well, she just took off. She wrote nearly every day in her journal and in her creative writing folder. It took a while, but eventually she even agreed to revise and edit.

She wrote about her mother and about her home. She wrote about her pets and her friends. She discovered poetry and the creative chord it struck in her.

She began to read every poem in the room and attempted to produce her own poetry from time to time. Since she was the oldest person in the room, her interests were a little different than most of the other children. As she wrote, she began paying attention to all the major elements of the mechanics of print and to spelling as well. And she began to self-correct things with which she wasn't satisfied. She wanted to write, and she wanted to do it "correctly". I was amazed. I was also very thankful that I had learned enough to see and value what Angel was showing me about her abilities and her learning rather than focusing on deficiencies.

In a draft of a story produced in November, she rejected her own lead and started her story another way. When the story was finally ready for publication, she had written seven drafts. Her writing was always purposeful. She wrote for a wide variety of audiences and explored several genres throughout the year. She become quite a creative storyteller and was recognized as such by the rest of the class. She stopped sucking her fingers and no longer seemed to feel like she didn't belong.

Angel worked very hard at revising and adding information so her readers could fully understand what she wanted to convey. Once, as she was rewriting, completely absorbed in her story, I heard her mutter to herself, "Now, let's see if this makes sense." I loved watching her develop, observing the process at work. And I thought, if it works for Angel it works for everybody.

Her reading improved along with her writing. As she gained confidence, she and I read together. When she finally read for me instead of with me, I found that she didn't skip unknown words and read on. She simply became stuck, hesitating for as much as a full minute or until I helped her. I asked her what she does when she comes to a word she doesn't know if I'm not there. "I put the book up", she confessed. I suggested that if she didn't want to put a book away she could try skipping the troublesome word. She could skip it, read to the end of the sentence, come back and then try the word again by starting to say the first part of the word. If that didn't help she could just put in a word that makes sense and go on. We tried that with several unknown words in *Aunt Flossie's Hats*, by Howard, one of her favorite read aloud books. She read it with my help, figuring out words and inserting meaningful substitutions.

She was surprised at how successful this strategy was. That was the middle of October, and by February she was reading nearly anything she wanted to read. Clearly, she already knew a great deal about print, but she didn't know how to make it work for her. Rereading, starting to say the word, substituting, and self-correcting became her special talents, and she explained how to be a better reader to many of the other children. As an older child, she decided it was her duty to help the other children. Actually, she was quite a good teacher, and her explanations and impromptu demonstrations about reading assisted more than one of her classmates.

By Christmas, Angel demonstrated her developing abilities as a writer with this Christmas message for the children in the kindergarten class with whom my second-graders worked.

Merry Christmas to all—Ho! Ho! Ho!

by Angel

Christmas is coming so you best be good. Don't ask me why because you'll soon find out.

You can get many things like. . . airplanes, cars, bikes too. Clothes, shoes, toys too.

You may get real animals too. Don't get your hopes up or he might not come see you.

Get up in the morning and open your presents. Go places.

Eat Christmas dinner with your family. There are many things to do.

Have a wonderful time.

The End

Most of the words were spelled conventionally in the first draft. Punctuation was accurate. She was even experimenting with an ellipsis. While the sentiments expressed in the message reflect her hope of good things to come, they also reflect her experiences, her fear that wanting things results in arbitrary denial or even punishment. Such cautionary expectation is a common emotion for these children. Angel doesn't only tell her readers to be good. "Don't get your hopes up", she warns, "or he [Santa Claus] might not come to see you."

Toward the end of the school year, we had a celebration day. The children displayed their work, some of the books they published, their projects, and favorite art. They wrote and produced a play and planned a party down to the last detail. They made the invitations, and I arranged for the refreshments. Several of the children's parents came, many of whom had never been to the school before. Angel's mother was among them. As Angel danced to a Chopin polonaise (the children liked Chopin best of all the classical composers we heard that year), her mother started to cry. When the play was over, she thanked me. She told me how grateful she was. She never thought Angel would have such a good year in school. "Angel is so happy, and she has learned so much. She brings books home, and she really reads them", her mother told me. "She enjoys school."

Lynn was another of my students that year who helped me decide I was finally on the right track as a teacher. Lynn came from an overcrowded classroom during the second week of school. She was terrified. She was shaking and crying when they brought her to our room. I had to just sit and hold her for a long time and talk to her. While Angel quickly decided to try new things, Lynn was the least risk-taker I'd ever had. She never wanted to write, and when she did write she'd become so frustrated she'd almost cry.

Everything she produced for months sounded stilted and like a pre-primer story. She just would not venture beyond repetitive, short choppy sentences. "I like my Mom. Do you like my Mom?" "I like school. Do you like school?" She almost never used a word she couldn't spell. When she really wanted to write a new word, she'd stop and look it up. I was beginning to think she would never get beyond those short, nearly meaningless texts. I kept thinking that maybe I should force her to write something else; then I'd think that maybe this is what she needs. Maybe she's telling me she needs time, time to practice and to feel safe. She is, after all, writing predictable, repetitive stories. That's good for beginning readers, I reasoned. Perhaps it's good for some beginning writers, too. It isn't always easy to see the strength or the positive message in what the child is doing. I didn't know whether to push her into other areas of writing or let her stay where she was for a while longer.

Once in October, I saw her laboring over a text and asked her what she was writing about. She said "A jet plane". We were reading Robert Munsch books, and I had just shared *Angela's Airplane* with the group. I thought, "Oh, wow, this is going to be a different story." But that was not the case. I was disappointed because Lynn had merely substituted the word jet for Mom or school in her standard format. "This is a jet. Do you like my jet?" and so on. But then I realized this story was more elaborate than her usual attempts. Although not a huge leap, it still represented some growth.

Again, I wondered if I should require her to try something more or let this patterning continue a little longer. I could see that she was teaching herself how it all works, but at the rate she was going I might be retired before she wrote one original, complex sentence. I told myself this just isn't working. All my encouraging, modeling, inviting, and all the sharing we were doing wasn't getting through to Lynn. She was blithely going on her way writing for the pre-primer audience, and this was second grade.

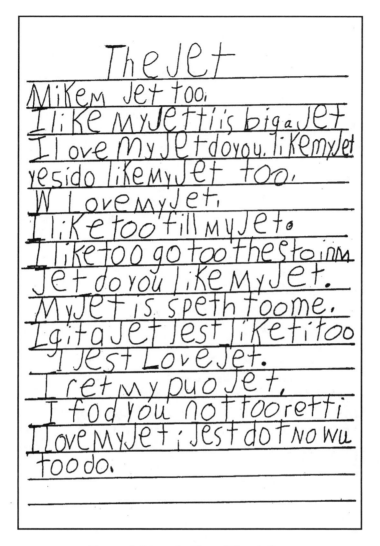

Figure 3.2 Lynn's Story "The Jet"

Lynn was struggling with reading too. She was so bound up by the phonic drill she'd had in first grade that she tried to sound out every word, even "t-h-e". She couldn't think about what she was reading or try to read for meaning using what she knew about language, because she was so focused on letter-sound relationships. I did a lot of assisted reading that fall with children like Angel and Lynn. When I'd ask Lynn to read alone, she'd literally try to sound out every word. That was the only thing she knew to do. That was her understanding of what reading was. There was virtually no evidence of predicting, and she couldn't remember a "new" word from one page to the next, even when it was repeated several times. I really didn't know what to do.

Gradually, as we read together and talked about how reading works, she began to approach reading as a language and meaning making process. In my conference log on Lynn, dated January, I noted that she "recognizes most common words in context" at this point. She could "retell a story" by then and she "initiates reading on her own", rather than only when it is SSR time. During those January conferences she selected and read several good books including DePaola's *The Popcorn Book*, as well as *The True Story of the Three Little Pigs* by Scieszka, and *Love You Forever* by Munsch. I noted evidence of self-corrections and meaningful substitutions. She was understanding what she read. She laughed at *The True Story of the Three Little Pigs*. She took *Love You Forever* home to read to her mother. She suggested that we might make popcorn in class after reading *The Popcorn Book*. I reread my notes from conferences with Lynn and was amazed. I wrote about my despair over her lack of progress, and yet when I looked back, there was evidence of tremendous growth right there in front of me; I just didn't see it as it was taking place.

In February, Lynn wrote a story that was her breakthrough piece. It was about the death of her cat. In it, you hear Lynn's voice telling the story. This story is very different from anything she had attempted to that point. That's why I saved it. It reminds me that children need time. They will grow and make progress if they are allowed time and the opportunity to choose their own topics in writing and their own pursuits in reading. All that observing eventually paid off. It taught me about children like Lynn.

I know more now about when to insist that a child stretch out and try something new and when to support a child's repeating the same patterns. When it's clear to me that the learner is really engaged and almost transfixed by the pattern, I leave him or her alone for a while. When I come to believe that a learner is "faking it", then I push him or her gently into new arenas. Once in a while I have to say to a child, "No more 'I love you. Do you love me?' stories. Try writing something about yourself perhaps, or write an information piece about something we've been learning."

Figure 3.3   Lynn's Breakthrough Piece "My Cat"

Lynn wrote several information pieces during the spring. She would re-search a topic and then write an account of what she'd learned. She especially liked animals. In March, she wrote one of the stories that has become a favorite for me. It was "kite day", and she used that real event as a springboard to create a piece of fiction. I told her that's what writers do. I was very proud of her. As you can see from this draft, Lynn is taking several risks. She is using dialogue and many other conventions in her writing. She also self-corrects in that she marks out and erases. She writes good description and is beginning to exhibit confidence in her own abilities. Her developmental spellings show evidence of real learning. In just six months, Lynn has grown from a terrified child for whom school was frightening and painful, to a little girl who is beginning to think of herself as a successful writer, reader, and learner.

A Kite on a Rope
by Lynn

I fly my kite. I like to fly my kite. I fly my kite and it gets so high. It gets on top of Mrs. Childress' portable and I have to bring it back. My kites says, "Get me down, I am scared." Sometimes I say, "I can't get you down", and my kite starts crying. Then I say, "Stop crying kite. If you can't get down by yourself, I will come and help you. And I will talk to you until you get down." Then my kite isn't sad any more.
The End

Lynn didn't realize that her story was really about herself and her year in my classroom, but I knew. Personal engagement, supportive feedback, and time were the key ingredients for Lynn. Of course, I read with and to Lynn a great deal that year. I employed clozure activities because at first she didn't use meaning or grammar cues; she didn't seem to apply her prior knowledge or look at the pictures when she read. She was stuck in sound-it-out as her only strategy. We also did a lot of guided reading. And I let her write. I let it be hers, her process. That's what I learned. I can set it up. I can offer guidance, encouragement, instruction, and support. But I cannot do it for her or for anyone else. Learning takes place in the minds of the learners. They have to want it, and they have to make the necessary connections. I show them how to do that.

Gerald didn't even know he could learn when he first came to me. He had nearly failed first grade and was a very unhappy child when he entered my room in August. At first he was shy and quiet. His eyes downcast, he'd hang his head and thrust his hands in his jeans pockets. This was Gerald's typical stance. He couldn't read very well, and he wouldn't write at all, even in his journal. He appeared depressed, but I couldn't tell very much about him because he was so withdrawn. However, I soon discovered that, when invited, Gerald was a teller of great stories.

Sometime in early September, during a morning debriefing, someone asked if Gerald could tell about a shooting in his neighborhood. Apparently, he had been whispering the story to some of the boys. He was very upset by the event and told the story in gruesome detail. Afterward, the children encouraged him to write his story so we could have it as a class book that everybody could read. He agreed and took his pencil and a notebook to the back of the room where he wrote continuously for nearly an hour. When he was finished, all the children gathered at the rug for the reading of Gerald's story, even though they had just heard him tell it an hour before.

The Dead Man

by Gerald

He got shot in the horet 3 tims and shot in the legg and brock hes arm The poles came and the amlins came
Evre bode rad after the poles to see what wus going on. Thay see shuting and blud.

he is going to hav a frunr. thay is going to crie then they is going to go home. Thay proble dot have a penny. thay is proble por.

Soon as I got home I herd a bout it. This boy tod me about it then I rod a book about it. My claas love it. it is vere good.

they is going to set bie the frie and tok a bout it. it is going to be sad. thin thay is going to rest.

the man that celd hem is bad. I hate hem. if I see hem I am going to col hem a name. I gest hat hem so bad. The ples is looking for hem. wen thay cech hem thay is going to put hem be hin bares. sum one is going to paay his way out. I hat him! I hat him! I hat him! I hat him!

The End

Gerald wrote his story with the same feeling he displayed during the telling. He decided that he didn't need to remind his reading audience who the story was about. So he began, after identifying himself as the author, with "He got shot . . ." Gerald's story was eventually edited and published as part of our classroom library. The children loved this book, and Gerald's authoring career in my room was launched. He told and then wrote many wonderful and exciting stories that year. It took a while for him to appreciate the fact that someone who hadn't heard him tell them might want to read his stories. So we worked on audience and introductions during the first part of the year.

When he told and then wrote a story, it was always eight, ten or twelve pages long. He quickly came to think of himself as an author. His reading improved as well, but primarily, Gerald wanted to write. It was as if he'd had too few opportunities to express himself in his life, and the words just came pouring out. During the year, he wrote letters to his pen pal and other friends, kept a journal, and he wrote a collection of raps.

By our end of year conference, Gerald was doing very well. He was quite proud of himself. I helped him write to his favorite author, Tomie DePaola, to thank him for his wonderful books and to tell him how his books had helped Gerald learn. In that letter Gerald told Tomie, "I can read so good cause I write so much." Working with children like Gerald, I learned the importance of focusing on their strengths, interests, and intentions. Gerald became a self-proclaimed storyteller, an author, and a rapper in my classroom. The other children agreed. Shy and depressed at the beginning of the school year, he soon came to view himself as competent, and then as intelligent and talented. As his confidence grew, he took on greater challenges on his own. He also appointed himself the official greeter for the classroom. He came to believe that he could do all sorts of things well, and he was right.

SUMMARY

All three of these children live in poverty. None had a father in the home. Each child lived in federally subsidized housing projects. All had seen their share of crime and violence. They each frequently came to school upset about something that happened in the neighborhood. They all wore old clothes, often too small to be comfortable. They were all very thin as if they really didn't have enough to eat. To most of us, these children would not initially appear to be good learners. From a certain point of view, none were "ready" for second grade when I got them. But they blossomed. They turned their lives around during that year. They came to understand something about their own potential. They developed confidence in their own abilities. They not only learned to read and write better than I ever thought possible, but they learned to love learning and to like school. And they weren't the only ones. I watched children in that class learn things and come away with abilities and information I didn't know second graders could acquire.

Like all teachers, I was concerned about the standardized achievement tests. I didn't know if my students would do as well as those in more teacher directed classrooms, since I was spending virtually no time drilling on discrete skills that actually make up a large portion of test items. Theoretically, the students should be fine. After all, we can't read or write anything without using and working with all those skills. It's just that when we really use them they are integrated, and we aren't aware of them in isolation.

I need not have worried. My students did fine. They scored as well or better than the other second or third grade students in the school. They also scored comparatively high on certain aspects of the tests such as listening, knowledge of the environment, reading comprehension, and math. Each successive year has proven to be the same. My students do as well or better than their counterparts in more typical classrooms. And there is ample evidence of growth that is not measured by standardized tests. These include such data as their writing development, growth in spelling, vocabulary development, interest in current events, and the fact that they grow immensely in their ability to self-correct when they read.

A supportive classroom rich in language, literature and content focuses on making meaning with a purpose, and engages children in personal experiences with reading, writing, and learning. It allows them to see themselves as learners. These children came to believe in themselves and to think of themselves as growing in capability and competence. And most important, they came to see some of the very real possibilities for their own futures. Over the years I have learned more about how to plan for individual children, how to offer the open invitation to explore topics of their own choosing. I have improved how I integrate subject areas and how I identify learner strengths. I know more about how to support their growing reading and writing strategies. I know more about how to teach them so they overcome specific difficulties. I have come to realize that so much of what we call instruction, what we do with kids in terms of workbooks and lesson and programs, is meaningless. When we teach skills in isolation, they are difficult to learn and generalize from. Using a learning process teaches the children, but it also teaches the teacher. I continue to learn from my students, from other teachers, and from professional reading. And I continue to have a good time in the process.

References

Cambourne, B. (1986). *The whole story*. Portsmouth, NH: Heinemann.

DePaola, T. (1978). *The popcorn book*. New York: Holiday House.

DeVeaux, A. (1987). *An enchanted hair tale*. New York: Harper Collins.

Diamond, B. & Moore, M. (1995). *Multicultural literacy: Mirroring the reality of the classroom*. White Plains, NY: Longman.

Howard, E. (1991). *Aunt Flossie's hats (and crab cakes later)*. New York: Houghton Mifflin.

Kozol, J. (1991). *Savage inequalities: Children in America's schools*. New York, NY: Crown Publishers.

Climo, S. (1989). *The Egyptian cinderella*. New York: Harper-Trophy.

Mendez, P. (1989). *The black snowman*. New York: Scholastic.

Mullis, I., Campbell, J. & Farstrup, A. (1992). *Executive summary of the NAEP 1992 reading report card for the nation and the states: Data from the national and trial state assessments*. Washington, D.C.: Office of Educational Research and Improvement, U.S. D. O. E.

Munsch, R. (1988). *Angela's airplane*. Ontario, CAN: Firefly Books, Ltd.

Munsch, R. (1988). *Love you forever*. Ontario, CAN: Firefly Books, Ltd.

Numeroff, L. (1985). *If you give a mouse A cookie*. New York: Harper & Row.

Peterson, R. (1995). *Life in a crowded place*. Portsmouth, NH: Heinemann.

Short, K. & Burke, C.(1992). *Talking about books*. Portsmouth, NH: Heinemann.

Strickland, D. (1994). Educating African American learners at risk: Finding a better way. *Language Arts. (71)*,328-335.

Taylor, D. (1991). *Learning denied*. Portsmouth, NH: Heinemann.

Chapter 4

"Try Huff and Puff!": Discovering Children and Creating Curriculum in One Small Town Third Grade

Cathy Clarkson

Several years ago an experience with a young child reminded me as nothing else could just how important teachers can be in children's lives. *Rachel* is a Down's Syndrome child. By seven years of age, she showed no progress with language and seemed content not using language to communicate. The school staff was resigned to the fact that she did not speak, but her parents were devastated, believing they would never be able to talk to their little girl and learn what she thought, what she had to say. The staff told Rachel's parents they should learn to use sign language. When she was placed in my class, no encouragement was offered that she would or could learn to communicate with speech.

I believe in classrooms that immerse children in both oral and written language, but I didn't know if this environment would benefit Rachel. Early in every school year I read favorite fairy tales with my third graders. The children are usually very fond of all the variations of "The Three Little Pigs". We spend as long as two weeks reading and exploring *The Three Little Pigs, The True Story of The Three Little Pigs, The Fourth Little Pig, The Three Little Havelina's,* and so on. I wasn't sure how much Rachel was getting from the stories, but she seemed to be enjoying herself. She'd listen when I read, and she'd attend to what the other children were doing: role-playing, drawing, writing, reading aloud, discussing illustrations and storyline differences and similarities, etc.

One afternoon, following a dramatized version of James Marshall's *The Three Little Pigs*, the class went for a bathroom break and water. As I was gathering the children in the hall by the drinking fountain, I realized Rachel wasn't among them. I went into the girls' bathroom to get her. As soon as I entered, I realized she had locked herself in one of the stalls. These stalls had long doors so the children could not lock the door from the inside and then crawl out. Unfortunately, that meant I couldn't crawl in to get her, so I started talking to her. I asked her to come out. I asked her if anything was wrong. I tried to assure her that no one was angry with her, and that nothing would happen to her if she opened the door.

The more I talked, with no response and no movement on her side, the more concerned I became. I pleaded, "Rachel honey, please open the door." I heard nothing. At some point I changed my plea to "Rachel, Rachel, please, let me in. Let me in." Then I saw one little eye peering at me through the crack between the door and the frame. Again, I implored, "Rachel, let me in. Let me in." I continued pleading until, from the other side of the door, I heard a throaty little whisper, "Try huff and puff."

"What?" I asked in disbelief. She repeated her request. "Try huff and puff," she said, louder and stronger this time. I ran into the hall and told the other children that Rachel was talking. I explained that she had locked herself in the bathroom and told them she wanted us to "do" *The Three Little Pigs*. All the children crowded into the girls' bathroom and helped tell, complete with different voices for each character, the story of *The Three Little Pigs* with Rachel playing the third and smartest pig. At the end, when the big bad wolf was finally banished, never to be heard from again, Rachel opened the door and came out to the cheers, applause, and hugs of her classmates.

I see Rachel every so often out shopping with her parents. Although she is older now, she always has a smile and a hug for me; and while she continues to have many problems, she has never completely stopped talking. Her mother and I both get tears in our eyes when we speak of the day Rachel had us tell the story of "The Three Little Pigs in the Girl's Bathroom".

I never taught "by the book" and, after my experience with Rachel, I knew I never would. I always worked to form a community in the classroom. That is usually fairly easy given the nature of the small town/rural surrounding of the school in which I teach. I always understood the need to have a community of learners, but now I am much better at helping the children become a community of people who care about and for each other. While we study much of the content of the third grade curriculum, we do it in our own way, and we always add so much to it. Most of what we do is read, read, read, and write, write, write all day. Except for the 45 minutes we spend on math every morning, the remainder of our day revolves around learning science, social studies, and literature in the context of theme cycles. Our art, music, computer, etc., support learning and the self-expression grows out of these units.

For the past few years, I've also involved my students in a variety of celebrations, rituals, and ceremonies (Peterson, 1995). We always did morning routines and celebrated birthdays, but now we have several rituals throughout the day. We celebrate all sorts of other important days as well. We make cards and do farewell cheers when one of the children moves away, and we make a production out of presenting our cards and telling the child who's leaving what we will miss most when he or she is gone. We exchange home addresses, phone numbers, and e-mail addresses. We also make cards for new arrivals. We present our cards to the new child in a welcoming ceremony, and each student says something they are looking forward to doing with the new addition. The children, however, decided that we couldn't make cheers for new kids because we didn't know them yet, and "didn't know the important things to say."

Now I have established patterns that I implement beginning on the first day of school in the fall. I begin each school year, usually on the first day, by reading my favorite books. I pile up several books in the middle of the rug and we sit in a circle, and I share. Then I display them on a shelf labeled "Ms. Clarkson's Favorite Books". I show them how old and worn some of my books are. As I read I tell them stories about why this or that book is a favorite. For example, my grandmother read *Tikki Tikki Tembo* to me, or *Goodnight Moon* is a favorite because I read it to Sam, my son, when he was little. I thought every child had heard *Goodnight Moon*, but many children haven't. I read *Miss Nelson is Missing* because that was Sam's favorite bedtime story when he was in kindergarten. I read *Curious George* because that is my daughter, Lilly's, favorite book now. I used to read *Strega Nona* to the children because I love folk tales, and it is one of my favorites. But now, although it is in the display, I usually save it for our Tomie DePaola author study. I tell the children that we will read this book later in the year, so they'll be looking forward to it.

Starting on day two, they are asked to bring in their favorite books from childhood. We make another pile on the floor and sit in a circle and read for most of the morning over the next three or four days. This sets the tone for our approach to books and to reading for the rest of the year. We continue to read and share our favorite books. The children can bring in any books they love. Some of them bring in baby books because they loved them when they were little, and we talk about the emotional ties we have with books and how your heart feels when you see a certain book. Some of the children nod their heads and understand that their favorite books make them feel good.

The children who have never been read to don't have any idea what I am talking about, at first. Some of the children don't have any books to bring in. So I always ask the kindergarten and first grade teachers what books the children seem to like best, and I keep a collection of those titles in the room during the first few weeks of school. The children who come with no books at all can look through our classroom library and bring to the pile a favorite book or two that they remember from kindergarten or first grade "when they were little". I try throughout the year to encourage a love for good books. It doesn't take long before all the children have favorite books that they want to share and display. Even in the late spring, some of the children are still bringing books from home. All of them have trade books at their desks.

On the second or third day of school, in the fall, we begin to write about our favorite books. That is how I set up their Writer's Notebooks at the first of the year (Calkins, 1995). We write about our memories, our favorite parts of the book, what we would like to write about, what we want to know about, and so forth. This progression is very successful but I have to model new entries in my Writer's Notebook, initially. I have been keeping one of my own for years that I use as a demonstration.

Next, we move into a class literature study. By the beginning of the second week of school, I usually have started reading a chapter book to the class. Lately, I have begun the school year reading *The Boxcar Children*. Of course, I read aloud from several books everyday, and after I have shared a book, it goes into the free choice center for individual self-selection time. The children who have never been read to are usually the children who are the most at risk and the ones who struggle the most with school learning, especially reading and writing.

When I think of children who struggled this year, I think of *Becky*. Becky was labeled learning disabled and went to special education classes up to this year. She didn't really begin reading until last year, and she still reads slowly. Here is her first Writer's Notebook entry from last August.

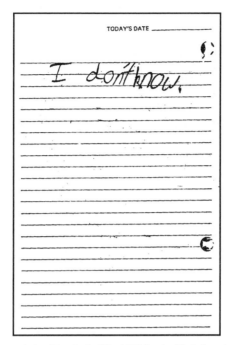

Figure 4.1   Becky's First Writer's Notebook Entry

We have worked on things like how to know when something doesn't make sense in your reading and strategies for self-correcting in both reading and writing. I encourage the children to write about everything in their Writer's Notebooks. Mine has notes, sketches, pictures, magazine and newspaper articles, cards and letters. The children usually find it fascinating, but Becky really got into keeping her own. She has come a long way in writing. Last month, she wrote about going to visit her cousin J.D. She actually said to me, "You know, there is a real story here".

Becky still believes in magic, in the magical world of childhood, and she talks about it and writes about it. We are reading *Charlotte's Web* now. When we were discussing Fern's understanding the animals, I asked the children if they thought Fern would ever lose her ability to talk to animals. Becky quickly said that she would. She knew this to be true, she told us, because right now she understands her dog's language, but nobody else in her family does. She said her sister used to, but she lost that ability when she got a boyfriend. Becky told me privately that you lose your imagination when you grow up, but that she wanted to keep hers.

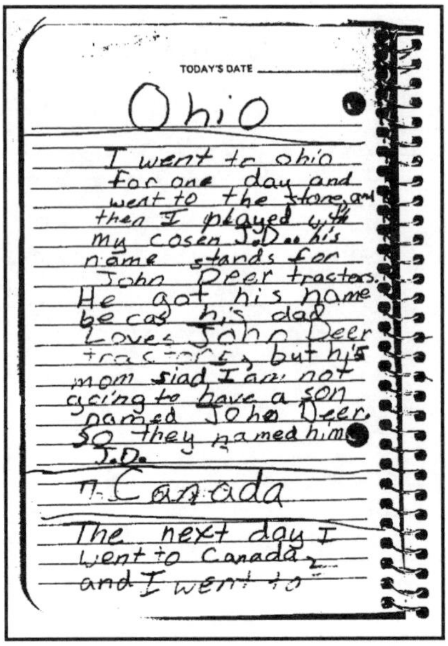

Figure 4.2   Becky's First Story

Becky had a hard time making friends at the beginning of the year because she was shy and lacked confidence in herself. But now she is sort of the leader of a group of girls in my class. They developed a complicated role-playing game and play it everyday at recess. It involves princesses and witches and knights and queens. I don't understand it, but I know it is very complex.

One day, this group of little girls found worms in the grass during recess. It had just rained, and they brought their worms into the classroom and put them in the terrarium. They said they had read you could do that, so they wanted to see. They wrote signs and named the worms; Samantha was one of the names. They said this was an experiment to see "if the book was right". They decided to check the next day to see if the worms were dead and dried up. Just in case they were, they asked all the other children to leave them alone. To date, the worms are wiggling away in our classroom terrarium.

Becky's self-confidence has grown tremendously this year. Her imagination is really valued and important in my classroom, and she knows it. She has found her voice and participates willingly in the life of the group, sharing information she has learned, reading favorite books, writing, creating games, asking good questions, and entertaining us with her unique take on life. Getting to know Becky has been a pleasure.

Lucas is a different story. Lucas's reputation preceded him. The whole school knew that he was uncooperative and had a surly attitude. Because I knew about him, I was ready to make a special effort to include him in our classroom community. In the beginning, there were many days when it was difficult to even like Lucas, but I have come to like him very much. Here is one of his first written messages from the beginning of the year.

Figure 4.3   One of Lucas' Early Messages

What Lucas had to learn was that I would give him a chance, and that has made all the difference. Every six weeks, the students change groups so that each child works with nearly every other child in the room sometime during the year. At those times, I ask the children to list two children they would like to sit by and one child they would not like to be with. I keep a chart of their requests so I know what is going on socially. I want to know if there are children who need extra protection or help being included.

Lucas did not believe I would honor his request. He knew he had been "bad" and thought I would punish him by making him sit with students he didn't like. But I gave him what he asked for. When I wrote the second six-week seating arrangement on the board, Lucas looked confused. He came to me and said, "Are you sure about this?"

That was the beginning. For Lucas to believe that a teacher would listen to him was a real breakthrough. Now he is joyfully included in groups with other students, and he shines in drama activities. When I told his mother that he is good at drama, she was astounded. Lucas has decided that he wants to take drama classes this summer. He jumps on anything positive about himself.

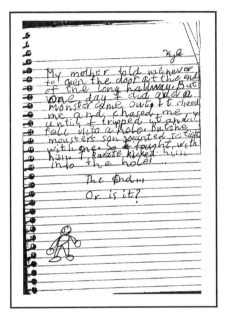

Figure 4.4   Lucas' Writing

He still has his moments, but he no longer has whole days that are out of whack. Now he feels like he belongs, and he is a different child because of that.

Caitlyn is another child who came into her own through classroom drama. At the beginning of the year, Caitlyn's mother told me that "Caitlyn doesn't talk to teachers", and I found out that it was absolutely true. She only whispered to her classmates. At first, Caitlyn attempted to communicate with me through messengers. She would send other children to me with her questions. When I refused to answer them, she eventually came herself, whispering in my ear and averting her eyes.

When we had our first classroom drama, Caitlyn whispered to me, "Do I have to do that?" and I whispered back, "Yes, you do." I told her she could choose any part and be anything, but she had to try. As the year has progressed, so has she. She's been involved in drama activities and projects with groups of students, and she has come out of her shell more and more. It didn't take long for her to find out that it was safe, fun and that she liked participating. Just like a movie star, one or two critically acclaimed successes and she was on her way. As soon as Caitlyn started really talking, some of the children told her teacher from last year, "Caitlyn is talking now, aren't you glad?"

The other thing I discovered about Caitlyn was her love for writing. She fills entire notebooks. According to her mother, "She is always writing". At the beginning of the year, her writing looked immature, like a first grader's, but it didn't take long for that to change, too.

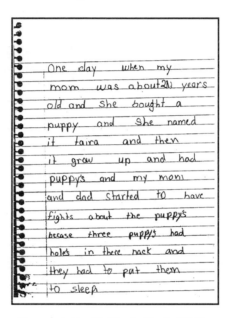

One day when my mom was about 2ll years old and She bought a puppy and She named it faira and then it graw up and had puppy's and my mom and dad started to have fights about the puppys becase three puppy's had holes in there nack and they had to put them to sleep

Figure 4. 5   Caitlyn's Early Writing

By the end of the first semester, she was writing longer, more complex stories with bigger words and more complex sentences. She also discovered the virtues of revising and editing. She has made great progress this year.

	About a Kitten
●	One day I was going to wall paper my
	room and I wanted to have horses on
	my wall. My mom wanted me to have
	Kittens on my wall paper she said if
	you get that wall paper I'll buy you a
	Kitten. Then I liked the wall paper and
	it toke us for weeks to find kitten. My
●	mom said "What kind of kitten do you
	want? I wanted a calico so we tried
	looking for one, but we could not find
	one. Then I want a Himalayan, But we
	could not find one. My mom said "Do
	you want a persian?" And I said yes.
	She looked in the news paper and she
	did not find one She saw where call a
●	girl and she had nine of them. My
	mom got her number and she called

●	her. and my mom said comeon were
	going to got pick out a kitten. We
	got a black and white Kitten and
	the Lady said it was a girl but we
	Kept on going to the docters and
	my mom said to the docter "Is that
	a boy kitten? And he chacked and
●	it was a boy and it"s name is Oreo
	and he now jumps up the stairs and
	down the stairs and runs funny
	funny and fast when your still
	sleeping at 6:00 he comes and
	sleeps on your face, your back and
	your head. And he goes after your
	feet when your wiggle them. I love
●	my Kitten.

Figure 4. 6 Caitlyns Later Writing

Houston is another child who has also made remarkable progress this year. He qualified for special education in the fall, so he's out of the classroom part of the morning. But when he comes back, he just jumps right in to whatever we're doing. At first, he didn't really want to attempt to write, but when he did, we found out that he had such wonderful things to say. Here is a story he wrote in November about his grandfather. You can see his first draft and a revised, edited version. I thought this was a wonderful piece. The children all love to read Houston's stories.

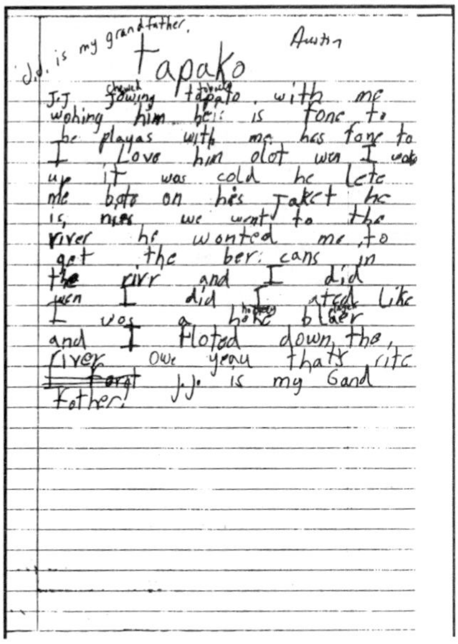

Figure 4.7
Houston's First Draft

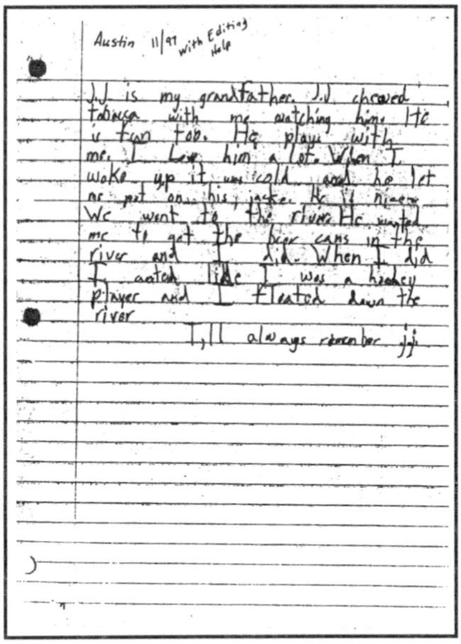

Figure 4.8 Houston's
Revised, Edited Verson

Then there's *Tony*. Tony is one of the most unusual and likeable children I've ever worked with. He and his family moved to Memphis last week, and we all miss him. Here is the entry he wrote the day he found out they were going to move.

Tony came to me on the first day of school in August and confided to me that he couldn't "read too good." He was able to call words, but he lacked confidence and was so focused on getting the words right that he lost meaning. He also lacked many of the experiences he needed to help him predict and construct meaningful text. But he tried hard. He has read a lot this year, keeping a chapter book or two at his desk at all times. His mother said that "he even asked for books for Christmas!"

Tony has great compassion for other children, and they lean on him for support, understanding, and encouragement even though he maintains the image of the "tough guy" as well. He pats his friends on the back when they need encouragement. He tells children who are upset that everything will be all right. He helps others with tasks that require physical strength.

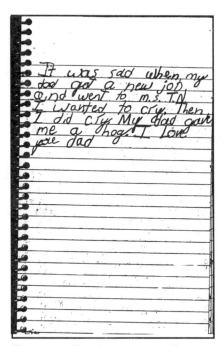

Figure 4.9 Tony's Notebook Entry

Tony has also gained confidence in his academic ability throughout the year. I try to get the children to write stories for the math facts they are having trouble learning. Since third-graders have to learn the multiplication tables, that means most of them could write stories for nearly every multiplication fact after 2 X 2. Tony discovered that he liked making up or paraphrasing stories for math facts. Here is one of his unedited stories, complete with developmental spellings.

3 X 3 = 9

There once was a mice that were about to have triplits. She was weried becase she had a cosen that was born with no tale. Her birthday came and to her delight her triples did not only have one tail but three tails each!

When we were reading biographies Tony came to me and said, "I know what I'm reading now, how about that?" Tony read a biography of Jim Thorpe and loved it. I always ask the children to keep a running summary of the biographies, so they have a record of some of the most important facts about their person. Here is a page of what Tony wrote from his book on Jim Thorpe. He was impressed with Jim Thorpe as a person and told me he thought life had been unfair to Jim.

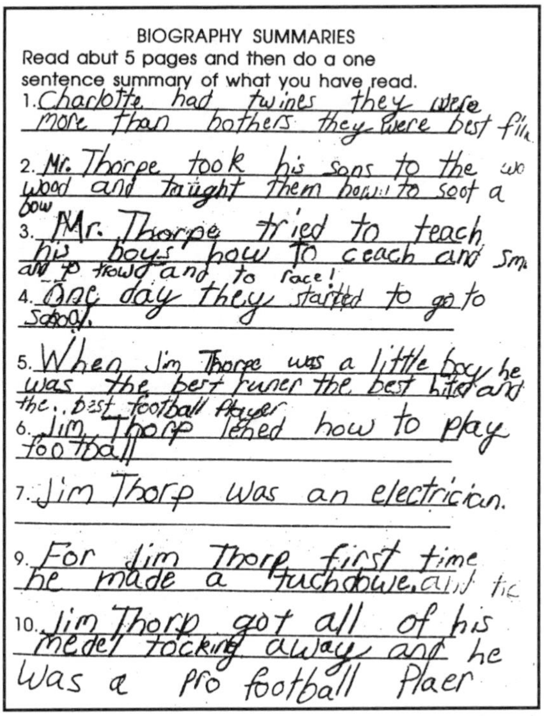
BIOGRAPHY SUMMARIES

Read abut 5 pages and then do a one sentence summary of what you have read.

1. Charlotte had twines they were more than bothers they were best fi..
2. Mr. Thorpe took his sons to the wood and taught them how to soot a bow
3. Mr. Thorpe tried to teach his boys how to ceach and Sm [illegible] trowd and to race!
4. One day they started to go to school.
5. When Jim Thorpe was a little boy he was the best runer the best hiter and the best football player
6. Jim Thorp lened how to play football
7. Jim Thorp was an electrician.

9. For Jim Thorp first time he made a tuchdowe, and tic

10. Jim Thorp got all of his medel tocking away and he Was a pro football Plaer

Figure 4.10 Tony's Facts About Jim Thorpe

Our class is still grieving over Tony's moving away. As always, we had a ceremony for Tony, presenting our farewell cards, singing goodbye songs, sharing our fondest memories of our time together and telling Tony what we will each miss most about him. On his last day Tony told me, "I hope my new teacher knows I'm good at some stuff." I hope so too, because he certainly is good at lots of things. I also hope our class left him with enough confidence in himself to sustain him in his new situation until he finds his niche. Many of the children have already written to Tony and are anxiously awaiting his replies.

It took me quite a few years to figure out that I had to have more than creative ideas and an intuitive ability to relate to children. I also had to have a plan, and I had to have some consistency in my daily classroom curriculum.

Every morning has established routines that include some talking together, making choices for the morning, singing songs, saying the pledge, changing the calendar, checking the weather, adding to our class time line, examining an aspect of language in writing, doing some activity that includes number concepts, and read aloud time. But I am most happy about what I have finally come up with for homework.

This is a school where the parents want and expect me to give homework. I believe the value of homework for young children lies as much in responsibility building as it does in what they are supposed to be learning. Consequently, I give some homework, but only twenty to thirty minutes a day. On Monday, the children have to complete a page from a phonics workbook. This is also a school where we are directed to teach a phonics program of some sort, and the parents demand that we do that. The parents are more comfortable if they can see some direct evidence that I teach phonics so I use this workbook. It has twenty words per unit representing two or three different phonic patterns. On Tuesday, I ask the children to write one sentence for each of their twenty words. On Wednesday they have to do six operations as practice for spelling those words correctly (write each one, close your eyes and visualize it, spell it from memory, etc.,) and all the parents are supposed to help. On Thursday I give them ten to twelve math problems practicing the math skill or concept we've worked on that week. They also have to take a practice spelling test that an adult in the home must administer. On Friday, we have our spelling test and no homework over the weekend.

Each week's homework follows the same pattern. Every morning, I check to see that they did it and if a child had trouble with any of it. Then, I work with that child until the difficulty is cleared up while the other children write, or read independently. Their homework is checked off and that's all. This patterned and limited homework schedule has solved several problems for me as a teacher. First, I never have a child say, "But I didn't know we had ___ for homework." Of course, we do more work with spelling and phonics in class based on their real reading and writing. But, the parents are happy because they believe in workbooks, and I am happy because I don't want to waste children's precious classroom time with arbitrary workbook exercises. Finally, I'm satisfied that I haven't overloaded the children or given them too much busy work.

However, what I did not anticipate was the improvement in their standardized test scores. Their spelling scores have gone up from an average of 3 and 4 stanines to stanines of 6 and 7 on the test given by the state. I am very pleased about that. The increase in test scores may be due to the added parent involvement. This simple and predictable homework schedule has perhaps been most beneficial for my at-risk students because they can handle it as well as everyone else.

Currently, I am getting ready to give my students this year's achievement tests and I am in the process of showing them the format issues and some of the things they ought to know to be testwise. This year my class is pretty wild, so I don't know how well they will do. Last year, after just the first few weeks of school, I could leave the room and the children would keep working quietly, often without realizing that I'd gone. But this year's group just isn't like that. I have to keep a closer eye on these kids. Every year is different. This year I have more children who are really struggling. They seem to come to school with fewer and fewer of the prerequisites that make for early success in school. But I have seen great progress this year among even the least proficient students, so I am hopeful they will do well on the tests.

I always have lots of letter writing in my classes, and this year is no different. We have written to favorite relatives who live far away. We have written letters-to-the-editor and letters to our local, state and federal representatives about issues that concern us. We have written many letters to favorite authors. One of the little girls wrote to Tomie DePaola. She told him how much she liked his books and that she especially liked *Oliver Button*. She said she liked the character because he stood up for what he believed. She told Mr. DePaola that she didn't know why she liked him until she thought about that book for a while. She said she liked people who stand up for what they believe. Another child's mother told me all her daughter wants to do is write letters. She said she was going to have to take out a loan for stamps and asked me if we were going to be moving on to some other type of writing in the next six weeks. I told her yes, we were going to explore writing information books, but that we would always write letters. The children really like letter writing. Some of them have started a class newspaper, and they also love making books.

The children direct most of their own projects and they keep units of study they really like going for long periods. This year, when we were learning about the solar system, three boys began a dialogue journal with each other. They talked about what planets they would visit and debated why life could or could not exist there. They looked up information to prove their points and ended up teaching the rest of the class a lot of details about each planet.

This group has especially enjoyed making their own alphabet and counting books from some of our units of study. I brought in all kinds of alphabet books, and the students brought in their favorites as well. We read and looked at them for several days. We started making alphabet books for one of the kindergarten classrooms that we partner with. Then, the children decided that we should make books for all the kindergarten and first grade classrooms and "spread it around". This year the children have made alphabet and counting books about pets, wild animals, insects, plants, endangered species, birds, the solar system, artists and colors to name a few.

The children make the rules for how class and projects are to be conducted. This year, several of the girls decided if a word has ever been in a book, even one time, then it is fair game for the alphabet books, but that the words had to come from books. The girls made that rule, and all the other children agreed. Then later, some of the boys decided they wanted to create an alphabet book of made-up names for jet fighter planes. They went to the girls and told them their book was going to be an exception to the rule. They discussed it, and the girls said that it was all right if the words were made-up for that particular book.

Initially, we spent two weeks working on alphabet books, but some of the children have kept them going during choice time. Even reading *Charlotte's Web* and doing all sorts of activities with that book hasn't completely ended their fascination with alphabet and counting books. Recently, some children have talked about doing an alphabet and a counting book using what they are learning about spiders.

When we started *Charlotte's Web*, one of the girls said, "Mrs. Clarkson, I already read that book". So I asked her if she had read it or if she had seen the cartoon film. She said she had seen the cartoon. I told her even if she knew the story, she would enjoy reading the book, especially the way we were going to do it as a class. Last week, she came to me and said I was right, that she had never heard the story the way we were doing it. I started by having them talk about friendship. We did friendship webs as the first event.

When I began reading the story, I also told them some information about E.B. White. They were sorry that he had died and that they couldn't write to him about his book. Some of the children wrote to him anyway because they just felt like they had to, they related to the story line and the characters so much.

I also found information on the Internet about both E.B. White and Garth Williams, the illustrator, and I found Garth William's obituary from a couple of years ago in the *New York Times*. We looked at other books he had illustrated, including the Laura Ingalls Wilder books. We studied his artwork and talked about what made you know a Garth Williams illustration when you saw one. Then I invited them to see if they could draw like Garth Williams—and they did. We put their illustrations out in the hall for a while, after each child selected the "perfect" piece of construction paper for mounting.

Several children said they would like to have written to Garth Williams, too, so I brought in two or three carefully selected samples of Dear Abby letters from the newspaper. We explored writing "Dear Abby" letters about the artwork, but then we got into writing letters about the story. We talked about letters Fern's mother might write and then one child wrote:

Dear Abby,
*   I live on a farm with my husband, my daughter Fern, and the animals. My daughter spends entirely too much time with the pigs. . . .*
*   Worried Mom*

Then many children wrote letters from Dear Abby back to Worried Mom. We edited the letters and posted them in a display so they could read them on their own. They were wonderful and full of sage advice like:

Dear Worried Mom,
*   Make her favorite dinner (not pork chops) and she will come home.*

One of my goals for the children is to show them that they can read chapter books on their own. After I read the first chapter book, such as *The Boxcar Children*, I only read the beginning of the next book. They finish it on their own and talk about it. Then we only preview the third book together before they read it individually and discuss it in small groups. Then they read another and another. Now they are reading *Charlotte's Web*, their fourth chapter book of this year. They are reading and discussing it mostly on their own with only minimal help from me.

Wanting to focus on character development, I had them stop at the end of the chapter where Templeton is introduced, and we talked about the character. Then they went back and wrote descriptors from the text and illustrated their list with drawings of Templeton. We mounted these on construction paper and put them in the hall to share with other classes because they were so good. The character of Templeton is so bad the kids just love him.

Sequencing the events in a story is one of the "skills" they are supposed to be able to do, so I have them do storyboards from stories. In *Charlotte's Web*, we do a storyboard experience when Wilbur escapes. Figure 4.11 is one shy little Caitlyn created. It was her idea to put the captions around the outside of each circle instead of underneath. These were wonderful so we put them on the back wall for everyone to see and read. The hallway and the regular bulletin boards in the room were full by then.

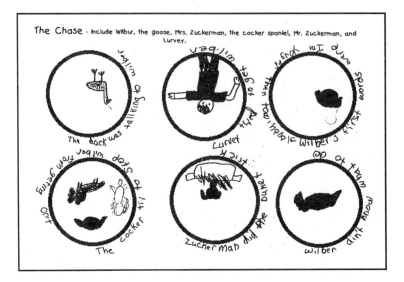

Figure 4.11 Caitlyn's Storyboard

Since we are finding out a lot about spiders from this book, now none of the children will kill a spider. They have a different view of life after getting to know Charlotte. That was one of the things I hoped to accomplish with this book, and I know my goal is being reached. We have written information pieces about spiders and made thumbprint spiders on them. The children have also written newspaper articles based on the book; "Tiny Spider Saves Big Fat Pig", and "Local Pig Narrowly Escapes Untimely Death". They came up with their own headlines and bylines. "Written by Licken Chicken" was one byline that I especially remember.

They also loved writing and learning about E.B. White. They have written about his life and discoveries about him that they found interesting. We have talked about his style of writing and looked at other books he has written. He has become a great favorite for some of the chidlren. We will talk about words that describe the people in *Charlotte's Web*. I'll ask them to come up with words to describe me. Then, I will give each of the children a small picture of themselves from their individual school pictures. I will make Polaroid photos for students who did not have school pictures taken. I'll suggest they put their pictures in the middle of their papers and then write words that describe themselves all around their photograph. We will mount the finished products on colored paper and make a display somewhere in the room.

We will complete at least one more literature study this year. I think the children want to read *Little House on the Prairie* next. We read *Little House in the Big Woods* in November. I always hope they will choose that book near Thanksgiving so we can cook the foods mentioned in the story and connect that with the holiday. We also have to finish our study of Van Gogh. I always have a mini-unit going on an artist or composer. We have studied Doc Watson, Chopin, Beethoven, Rembrandt, Monet, and now Van Gogh. Currently, the children are painting their own versions of "Starry Night". Van Gogh would be proud.

Every morning we have Language Workshop when we do our literature studies and our author studies—all the reading, writing and art. During that time, I also do whatever direct teaching about the reading process, written language conventions, skills and strategies I need to do. Typically, I use a big book to demonstrate whatever skill or strategy they need. For instance, this year I used *The Sunflower that Went Flop* by Joy Cowley to explore pronouns with the children, and then we wrote stories with lots of pronouns. I read *Why Can't I Fly* by Ken Brown to examine verbs, and recently I used *If You Give a Mouse a Cookie*, by Laura Numerhoff, to sort of revisit and highlight sequencing and predicting. I have found that using big books in third grade for direct teaching is really effective.

I also keep plenty of science and social studies based literature available in the classroom so I can expose the children to good books and provide them with opportunities to learn during their independent reading. I also try to read aloud to them from books that connect to what we are learning. We learned about George Washington Carver starting with Aliki's *A Weed is a Flower*, and that launched our study of biographies. When we were working on simple machines I read the poem "John Henry" to them, and we sang the ballad and wrote sequels to it. We read *The Magic School Bus Lost in the Solar System* at the beginning of the theme study on the planets and the solar system.

Every year is different, but I tend to do some things year after year because they are so successful. Before school is out this year, I hope to engage the children in an author study of Bill Peet. We will read *Big Bad Bruce, Chester the Worldly Pig, Huge Harold, Jethro and Joel Were A Troll, The Wump World* and many of his other books. If I do a Bill Peet author study, I do it late in the school year because most children can't read his books independently until then. Some of his books are complicated, and the children don't always get the humor. So I wait till toward the end of third grade to introduce them to Bill Peet. But when I do, they love him! They will be so excited when they find out that his is alive and they can actually write to him.

We have already done three author studies, Tomie DePaola, James Marshall, and Robert Munsch. I did Robert Munsch early in the year. Struggling children find a friend in Robert Munsch. They can read his books once we share a few, and all the children love them. This year, the children especially loved *Murmel, Murmel, Murmel*, and *Mortimer*. They wanted to write to him of course, and we also tried to write like him. They noticed elements in his writing that characterized a Munsch book. They discovered, among other things, that he likes to use the word "enormous" and he likes the number "seventeen".

But it isn't all wonderful books and joyful learning. Now that standardized test time is here, I think about grading and end of year reports to parents. I keep a journal about the children. I do a Running Record on every child at least three times throughout the school year (Clay, 1985). I also do informal miscue analysis on kids who are the least proficient—kids I'm worried about. I do one early in the year to see if their reading strategies change over time. I score their writing holistically and turn that into grades, and I also give tests. I have spelling test scores and test scores on math. I have some grades on homework, and test scores on vocabulary and science and social studies information. I also have the children assess some of their own written work and projects, and we turn those into grades. Then they assess their own learning. They look at their math, reading, and writing from the first of the year to the end of the year, and that seems to be really powerful for most of the children. They are nearly all amazed at how much they have learned about writing, math, spelling, vocabulary, books and authors, artists and composers, science and reading. They are amazed, but I'm not. It's the same every year. No matter where they start, they end the year knowing so much, having grown in both skill and confidence. No matter how they start the year, most children end up loving school. And to help ensure that they realize how far they have come and how much fun we have all had, we do an end of year celebration week that involves, among other things, sharing our favorite books and stories, oral and written, from the school year.

During celebration week, we have an Author's Award Day where every student is given an award for some aspect of their writing: best beginnings, best characters, most scary, best endings, best illustrations, most descriptive, funniest, saddest, and so on. The children help come up with the categories and then vote by secret ballot. Our awards ceremony is like the Oscars. Someone presents, and the recipient is encouraged to make a little acceptance speech. Last year, one of the boys said, "I'd like to thank all the little people who helped me get where I am today." And one of the girls declared, with a catch in her voice, "This has been the best year of my life, since kindergarten."

For me, though each year is unpredictable in may ways, they are each in their own way "the best year of my life", too. I remember the children and what we were able to accomplish together. I remember many of the things they say and what I discover about how their minds work and how they view the world. I try to take what I learn from each year's class and inform my practice as a learner-centered, reflective teacher so that I keep growing and improving. And each year I collect more stories, sometimes poignant, but mostly hilarious that become part of what keeps me in love with teaching.

References

Aliki, (1998) *A weed is a flower: The life of George Washington Carver*. New York, NY: Simon & Schuster Children's Division.

Allard, H. (1977). *Miss Nelson is missing*. Boston, MA: Houghton Mifflin.

Brown, K. (90). *Why can't I fly?* New York, NY: Doubleday.

Brown, M. (1947). *Goodnight moon*. New York, NY: Scholastic.

Calkins, L. (1994). *The art of teaching writing*. Portsmouth, NH: Heinemann.

Celsi, T. (1992). *The fourth little pig*. Houston, TX: Steck Vaughn.

Clay, M. (1985). *The early detection of reading difficulties*. Portsmouth, NH: Heinemann.

Cole, J. (1990). *The magic school bus lost in the solar system*. New York, NY: Scholastic.

Cooper, H. (1988). *Homework*. Columbia, NY: Teachers College Press.

Cowley, J. (1982). *The sunflower that went flop*. Aukland, New Zealand: Shortland Publications, Ltd.

DePaolo, T. (1975). *Strega nona*. New York, NY: Simon & Schuster.

Marshall, J. (1989). *The three little pigs*. New York, NY: Dial.

Mosel, A. (1968). *Tikki tikki tembo*. New York, NY: Holt, Rinehart & Winston.

Munsch, R. (1985). *Mortimer*. Toronto, CA: Annick Press.

Munsch, R. (1982). *Murmel, murmel, murmel*. Toronto, CA: Annick Press.

Numeroff, L. (1985). *If you give a mouse a cookie*. New York, NY: Harper & Row.

Peet, B. (1977). *Big bad Bruce*. Boston, MA: Houghton Mifflin.

Peet, B. (1965). *Chester the worldly Pig*. Boston, MA: Houghton Mifflin.

Peet, B. (1961). *Huge Harold*. Boston, MA: Houghton Mifflin.

Peet, B. (1970). *The wump world*. Boston, MA: Houghton Mifflin.

Peet, B. (1987). *Jethro and Joel were a troll*. Boston, MA: Houghton Mifflin.

Peterson, R. (1995). *Life in a crowded place*. Portsmouth, NH: Heinemann.

Rey, M. & Rey, H. (1941). *Curious George*. New York, NY: Houghton Mifflin.

Scieszka, J. (1989). *The true story of the three little pigs*. New York, NY: Viking Kestrel.

Warner, G. (1950). *The boxcar children*. Chicago, IL: Albert Whitman.

White, E. B. (1952). *Charlotte's web*. New York, NY: Harper Collins.

Wilder, L. (1935). *Little house on the prairie*. New York, NY: Harper Collins.

Wilder, L.(1953). *Little house in the big woods*. New York, NY: Scholastic.

Chapter 5

"I Hate Words!"
Bridging the Gap with
Learning Disabled Fourth Graders

John E. Bertrand

I saw Jenni for the first time when she was working on a workbook of phonics exercises with a college intern at a desk out in the hall. As tears ran down her face, I heard her wail, "**I HATE WORDS! I HATE WORDS! I HATE WORDS!**" The college student was just two weeks into an undergraduate field experience. She looked shocked and at a complete loss. Clearly, she did not understand Jenni's difficulties.

The intern was patiently requiring Jenni to make her stumbling, halting way through several pages of exercises, and Jenni was unable to answer any of them correctly. It occurred to me that this little girl who said she hated words may just have decided that she would never be a reader. That possibility worried me because this was a special school for learning disabled children and a school of last resort for most of them. Some of the children had come here in kindergarten, after testing directly into special programs. Others, like Jenni, had failed in public school already, usually repeatedly.

Jenni was in the third grade and, as I later discovered, probably recognized fewer than fifty words. She had little awareness of sound-letter relationships or that words even consisted of separate sounds. But she liked this school because she was among other kids who all had learning problems, and she had teachers who cared about her and didn't humiliate her. She was in classes of 9 to 12 students, each with a full time teaching assistant. Nevertheless, Jenni wasn't learning to read and write.

But this school was beginning to change its educational philosophy and curriculum. It was moving away from a skill and drill, mastery learning sort of approach to a more inquiry and learner centered, integrated, literature-based program, and the effort was starting to pay off. Of course, the faculty had spent two years in decision making and curriculum development. The school had always had a good success rate with special children, but now it was an even happier place. The administration encouraged and supported the exploration into new ways of teaching.

The school intrigued me, so in my capacity as a university researcher, I offered myself as an informal resource. In that way, I became very familiar with the teachers and many of the students. I spent two mornings a week conducting a research project to study the process of teachers moving toward an integrated, literature-based program with LD and ADHD kids.

Jenni was in one of the classes I observed. I read to the children nearly every time I came, and they shared their work with me. I got to know them fairly well as learners. Jenni and the eleven other children in her class were truly learning disabled. Some of the children were hyperactive; some had attention deficit disorder; and one child was probably autistic. I learned a lot that year about the struggles of children with various learning disabilities and the teachers who try to teach them (Dudley-Marling, 1990; Poplin, 1988; Rhodes, & Dudley-Marling, 1988).

The research institute I worked for had been in decline for a couple of years in terms of state funding. When researchers left, they were not replaced, and I knew the day was soon coming when our "soft money" grant would end. I had been searching for another job for a while, and when I mentioned the fact to the director of the school, she offered me a job teaching fourth grade.

I jumped at the chance. I was given a room, fourteen students, one aide, and the freedom to teach as I saw fit. The director supported me in every way. She gave me a check to buy children's literature instead of basal readers and workbooks for the class. She saw to it that I got most everything I asked for, and she offered praise and encouragement on a regular basis.

I bought children's literature at the best bookstore in town, and we were off. I had been a teacher of elementary children at risk of school failure for a total of eleven years, but I had never taught a group where every child was learning disabled. The year I spent teaching fourth grade in this school was by far the happiest and most satisfying of my teaching career. This is the story of that year, told from the journals of three of the children and from my personal observations and reflections. It is a record of what the children learned and what I learned. We had a wonderful year.

KENT IN THE THIRD GRADE BEFORE MY YEAR WITH HIM

I am going to tell you about Kent in the third grade so that you will understand how defeated he was by school. I watched Kent two mornings a week for his entire third grade year as part of the study I conducted for the university. I recorded every move he made for as much as half an hour at a time, and in that process, two things became evident. Kent had limited literacy, and he was quite intelligent. In fact, he was a genius at covering up the fact up that he couldn't read or write very well. That had probably worked well for him in a large class in public school, but now he was in this special school with its small classes and one to five teacher-pupil ratio.

Kent rose to the challenge. He developed more multi-dimensional, involved, premeditated techniques to avoid schoolwork than any child I have ever seen. He was, in his own way, marvelous to watch. Certainly, avoiding learning tasks was not very good for him in long range terms, but in terms of immediate self-preservation, the native intelligence and cunning he displayed was impressive. He was the undisputed master of producing the least painful, short-term outcomes for himself. Kent had analyzed how this third grade classroom worked in detail and had devised ways to make himself as invisible as possible.

The teacher had invited me into her classroom to help her. She was beginning to employ real literature and to move away from total dependence on the basal program, but though her basic beliefs were in flux, she had not found the confidence to alter her teaching yet. She still spent most of her time in large group instruction and used the old directed reading activity lesson format with the new literature. She spent some time dealing with students individually, but students who were not being directly addressed were supposed to work on assigned seatwork, i.e., lots of workbook pages.

Kent played this system like a maestro. He appeared to be engaged, with much posturing, aligning papers, opening books, sharpening pencils, and so on. He rarely actually did anything, but he looked really busy. His act was not transparent; he truly appeared to be engaged any time the teacher looked his way or stopped by his desk to speak with him for a few seconds. She would look in on him between reading groups and during classwork times. He would appear intent on the work in front of him, and she would pass on.

Kent sat by himself in a corner of the room. The teacher told me that he distracted or interfered with any other child he was near. Clearly, he liked this seat, out of the teacher's normal line of sight, and had worked hard, from his point of view, to get it. His main nemesis was reading "group". He was the only member. So he could not hide, and he didn't like that at all. The rest of the time, he drew pictures, played games of his own devising, and talked to himself in whispers. I positioned myself nearby and listened. At length, I discovered that he was subvocalizing a fantasy world all his own as he told himself rousing stories.

As I reflected on my observations, I concluded that Kent was defending himself against what he perceived to be a hostile environment, one which conspired to make him feel badly about himself. His act was one of self-defense, and the result was that he had defeated every teacher he had encountered up to that time. Each one ultimately backed off and made the tacit deal that characterizes the school experiences of so many kids who have trouble learning. "If I leave you alone except when I have no choice, you will respond by making as little trouble in my class as possible. Deal?" Deal! As long as the "deal" was upheld, he found school tolerable. Of course, he wasn't making much progress. I timed Kent dozens of times over the course of that school year. At no time did he engage in a learning activity that required math, reading, or writing for more than 45 seconds.

KENT IN THE FOURTH GRADE

The next year I was Kent's teacher, and I braced myself. He was bright, desperate for positive attention and a sense of belonging, and he was still the best child I had ever seen at trying to remain invisible in the classroom. The first day of school, I commented to his dad how good Kent's verbal memory was. His father's face lit up and he said, "You'd never know he is LD at home. I can give him six or seven directions, each one dependent on the one before, and he will remind me what I forgot at the end of the day."

That first day I told the children that we wouldn't have many tests, and we wouldn't have any worksheets in this class. We would, however, read, and write about what we read, and draw about what we learned, and listen to each other talk about what we learned. I told them that we would not have many lessons with me at the board. I said they were going to learn about things that interested them and that they could work alone or in small groups, and I would be right there to help them.

Kent was thunderstruck. It was easy to see the wheels going around in his head as he considered this prospect. Of course, just to see if it was true, he trotted out all the old behavior patterns he had worked out in previous years. But, when a teacher wants to see your work, make suggestions, and sit with you talking and reading with you, it is difficult to pretend you aren't there. What was worse from Kent's point of view was that he had to make so many decisions himself: what to read, how long to take, what to write about, and so on. When school was no longer something the teacher imposed but something you had choices over and responsibility for, it became a very different game. For Kent, it was a scary situation.

Every morning, after I read to the class, we had rugtime. Then we went around the circle, and each child stated what he or she expected to work on that morning. One September morning, Kent proudly held up a book on about seventh grade level. "I'm going to read *The Prisoner of Zenda*," he proudly proclaimed.

Duncan snorted, "You're going to look at the pictures, you mean."

"Yeah, Kent", Ruth chimed in, "you can't read anything anyway."

I stopped them. "How many of you," I asked, "are expert readers?"

"Actually," I went on, "everyone here will be a reader at the end of this year." It was a promise they did not seem to believe, but Kent's face told me he very much wanted to.

"I will learn things too," I said, "because I will be reading and writing when you are reading and writing." They were completely unconvinced. Kent, however, looked thoughtful. "And the first thing I'm going to do is read this book every day with Kent. I read *The Prisoner of Zenda* when I was about fifteen, and I really liked it. Kent and I will both enjoy it." If it is possible to look complimented, relieved, and worried all at the same time, that is how he looked.

He spent those first few weeks trying in every way to avoid engaging with print. However, gaining the teacher's attention in positive ways by reading together for protracted periods is a powerful thing. We'd read together simultaneously, or I would read a paragraph, and Kent would re-read it.

At first, when he hesitated even a little, I told him the word. In this way, he could make it through a paragraph quickly enough to make sense out of it. Later, I explained to him. "Kent, most of the time, if you skip a word you don't know and read on then come back, you can figure it out. I will always tell you the word if you need it, but you have to try it first. And I'll bet you will be able to figure most of them out or put in something that is just as good." He remained skeptical.

I noticed that if I spent 30 minutes or more with Kent in the morning, he was much calmer during the rest of the school day. I was using a school-wide discipline system wherein children could earn and lose points for privileges, notably recess. Kent stayed in from recess three of the first four weeks. Finally, the Friday came when he received only one minus point for the week. At the end of that first good week, when I saw his mother coming to pick him up, I said, "Guess what! Kent only got one point this week; he can go out for recess everyday next week. Kent had a really good week. He worked hard and accomplished a lot." At first, his mother was speechless, and then she told him how proud of him she was.

Gradually Kent began to change. Some days, he was his old self, avoiding, making trouble, talking to himself, and full of anger. But, little by little, he began to engage for longer periods. He sternly refused to read books below fourth grade level, which of course meant that he always had difficulty and required my reading with him, part of the time. These were our guided reading and focus lesson times.

In November, he came to me and bitterly complained. "Jenni can read *Spider Goes to School* and I can't read anything. It's not fair; I work as hard as she does, harder even."

"Well, Kent," I said, " Jenni reads older level books with me and then practices on her own with easier books. Practice is important."

He was outraged and near tears. "But I can't read ANYTHING by myself," he shouted.

"Sure you can, Kent," I said, "Go get *Brown Bear, Brown Bear, What Do You See?*" Kent had not realized that he was slowly learning to read; that he had acquired new strategies in three months. Using picture clues, beginning sounds, knowledge of sentence structure, and the repetitive elements of this wonderful book, he read through with little difficulty. He was delighted, so I made a deal with him. If he would read three "baby books" every morning for practice, I would spend extra time with him whenever I could reading more difficult books. Kent made progress and the "baby books" he read increased in difficulty.

In January, Kent passed me a note to inform me that he had an important matter to discuss and wanted an appointment. I responded in writing, setting a meeting time and putting my response in his mailbox. His spelling was largely invented, but fairly readable. For the first time in his life he was writing for his own purposes.

When we met, he said, "The other kids don't like the Apple IIE. They all want to use the Macintosh. Can I learn to use the IIE so that I can have longer computer times?" I thought about it. There would be vociferous complaints from the more computer competent children if Kent got extra time. Computer time was at a premium in the classroom and jealously guarded. On the other hand, Kent was willing to do extra work to be able to use the older machine. I knew that he would have to learn a more complicated word processing program.

I asked him why he wanted extra computer time. "So I can write a book," he announced, "I am going to write my Robin Hood story." We had finished reading *Robin Hood* the month before, and he had tried to write a sequel and been defeated by the magnitude of the task. Writing was still a painful process for him, and I was amazed to learn that he had not abandoned this project. On the contrary, he had put considerable thought into how to solve it. He believed he could write if he had a computer. Only the old clunker in the hall was available, so he had made up his mind to master it. "Come on," I said, "I'll show you how to boot the program. It doesn't have a hard drive."

What a departure this was from the Kent I first encountered as the invisible student in the third grade. It was a major risk to try to learn how to use the IIE. Kent was still not reading independently past fairly simple books, but he was reading and writing every day. He was in a class where he was rewarded and praised for no more than his best effort. No one asked him to do things that he was unable to do, like sound out words from a list on a worksheet, and he never got graded until he was satisfied that he had done his best.

Kent finished the year reading roughly on a second grade level. He still encountered material that defeated his budding independence, and he worked slowly. But it was apparent that his parents had been right all along. He was not hyperactive in the conventional sense. School had been so painful for him that he had invented ways to avoid dealing with it.

One April day, I came back from a conference with a parent, my aide having been in charge of the classroom for an hour or so. Kent was at his favorite place, the old Apple IIE in the hall.

"Look at this, Mr. Bertrand," he yelled.

"Hold your voice down, Kent. What have you got?"

"It's a story about space pirates."

"Looks pretty good. Do you want some help with spelling?"

"Naw, I'll do it at the end of the period. But look, I've done three chapters." These 'chapters' were long paragraphs each.

"Excellent. Tell it to me?" He told me in some detail. I asked a couple of questions. We talked about what he might do in a revision or rewrite. But he wanted me to read what he had.

As I read the story, I suddenly realized that I was actually reading it. Some of the words were invented spellings, but Kent was an author! He was producing creative, interesting, lengthy, readable text. I was overwhelmed. It is days like that that remind me why I love teaching.

I smiled at him. "Kent, this is really good!" I said. "I am so proud of you." He gave me his characteristically charming smile.

Kent was growing and learning in school instead of falling farther and farther behind. By the end of the year, his anger and the avoidance behaviors had vanished altogether. His experience is a demonstration of the power of meaningful learning, of productive engagement within a print and content rich environment. He blossomed in a non-punitive atmosphere based on encouragement, inquiry, success, hard work, and the promise that trying would result in accomplishments that he himself chose and valued.

DAVY IN THE FOURTH GRADE

Davy arrived a day or two after the school year started. His parents had just been transferred to Nashville. In his old home, he had been in a public school, mostly in special programs. Davy was confident, self-possessed, and able to focus well on the task at hand. I could see at once that he would be no discipline problem. He listened attentively and was cooperative. He liked to read and had a well developed sense of narrative. Once during that first day, he whispered an explanation of what was happening in the story to a classmate who had momentarily lost the thread of the tale. It was also clear from the first that he was a sports fan. When he wanted an example to illustrate something excellent, he always compared it to a famous sports figure. When I distributed the newspaper to the class, he was the only child who requested the sports section.

I soon learned that he was indeed a very good athlete himself. That fall, he played soccer on a neighborhood team and was first string all the way. He also played baseball and basketball in season, and he talked about sports often. When the coach at a local university was fired and summarily replaced, Davy's opinions of the drama were as well thought-out as most adult comments I heard.

Davy read on or above grade level. His comprehension was appropriate to his age. He obviously liked a class where lots of reading took place, and it was only when I began talking about writing that his face fell. At the end of the first week, I discussed dialogue journals and response and observation logs with the children. I told them that I would respond to every entry every day. I had been wondering why Davy was in our school. As I spoke, Davy looked more and more uncomfortable. I soon saw why. For a boy who had such wonderful large motor control, he was truly a late bloomer in terms of small motor coordination. Watching him write was a dreadful experience. He tried as hard as he could to grip the pencil and control his hand, but it was of little use. No one could read what he wrote.

At rugtime that first week, I asked what he was going to read. He said, "I'm going the read *The War of the Worlds* by H.G. Wells. It looks great."

Then Lester said, "Oh, that's a good one. All these monsters come to earth and kill everybody. Wait till you see what kills them."

Then I asked, "How will you respond to this book, Davy?"

"Maybe I could draw a picture of the monsters," he said.

"Good, and what else?"

He began to look nervous. "And I could do a poster for the class."

"OK, will you also do a caption to hang on the poster explaining a little bit about the book or telling how you liked it?" I asked.

"Mr. Bertrand, I'm not too good with writing; could I do like a map instead?"

I said, " Davy, when you finish the book, I will help you write something about it. Don't worry, we will do it together." He didn't look happy, but he nodded.

Later that day, long before he finished his book, we began to put the spelling list for the week together. Children suggested words that they had encountered in their reading and writing, and I contributed a couple I had seen children have trouble with. Davy added two to the list. He obviously approved of this way of learning words we actually needed to know how to spell, and he participated enthusiastically. The crunch came when he had to copy the list off the board.

This can be difficult for learning disabled children. Some find it hard to translate a vertical to a horizontal surface. Others perceive letters on the board incorrectly. For Davy, it was difficult to write them at all. He was the last to finish. When Kent handed in his paper, I walked over to Davy. "Are you done?" I asked. He looked up, clearly uncomfortable, and I saw that he had only written half the words. In addition, he had copied all of them in between three lines on a college ruled page. I have never seen such tiny script. His words went up and down, none in line with the last. "Why do you write so small?" I asked. He shrugged and looked away. All his non-verbal behavior indicated how much he would like to be doing anything else.

"Well," I said, "we have to go on now. Stay in a minute when we have recess and finish your list, OK?" He literally sagged with relief, and I began to realize what a burden not being able to write was for Davy. Later, I came to understand that he was afraid... of being wrong, of being a disappointment to his dad whom he idolized, of being different, and worst of all, of being dumb.

"Wow, Mr. Bertrand," he gushed, "did you see where Michael Jordan might retire?" I nodded absently, trying to think how I was going to help Davy. "Maybe you'd like to write about that in your journal." I suggested.

We fell into this pattern. Nearly every day I found a way to encourage Davy to write. But he rarely took me up on it. After a few weeks I asked, "Why do you think writing is so difficult?"

"I don't know." He looked miserable.

"Well, I don't either, but one thing is clear to me. You've got to overcome it." I went on. "You know as well as I do, Davy, that school is going to be a problem for you until you write."

He nodded abjectly.

"OK, then," I said, "you and I are going to look for opportunities to write. You can write about what you know. You're a baseball player, Davy. How did you learn to throw a strike?"

He brightened up. "My dad painted a square of the strike zone on a wall, and I threw until I could hit it every time. I'm a really good pitcher."

"I know," I said, "and you got to be one through practice. This writing thing is the same deal, Davy. You have to practice every day."

"But I'm slow, and I can't make my letters. The other kids look at me when I am the last one to finish."

"Would you give up some of your free time if it meant that you could hand in your papers with the others? I could give your work back to you later, and you could finish." He looked doubtful.

"I don't know if I could finish even then," he said.

"Well, you try it. We'll see how it goes."

We went forward under this arrangement, and Davy was pretty good about it. But it was painful to watch. In an attempt to control his wandering hand, he wrote tiny script, bunched into little tight blocks. The sheer concentration of getting down a word at a time obliterated his comprehension, so he found composition impossible. In the end, he would compose a sentence, tell it to me, and then ask me to repeat it if he lost part of it as he wrote.

But he did improve. One day in January, I thought, "Is it my imagination or is Davy's writing getting a little bigger?" I looked at his journal again and then pulled out his portfolio for comparison. Not only was he improving, but he was writing much faster. The story he had written had been completed in four days, a vast improvement.

By the end of the year, Davy's writing had nearly tripled in size, and he wrote with comparative ease. It had been a long haul. At times, he was so frustrated that he could barely speak. On one or two occasions, he got in trouble by picking on another boy after a hard, discouraging writing project. He was such a rational child that a couple of explanations about displaced anger soon stopped those behaviors, but I heard his mother say on more than one occasion that some days he practiced baseball or soccer as if he were possessed by demons.

Progress was slow. If I had not been keeping a journal and portfolios of the children's work, I would have missed many of the wonderful things that were happening. Davy tried to write in a variety of ways, for many purposes, because that is how the classroom was structured, and through repeated efforts his approximations slowly gave way to more conventional forms. His speed and writing ability grew along with his self-confidence and sense of well being. This one year may just have given Davy back his chance to successfully participate in regular school and eventually to fulfill his potential.

JENNI IN THE FOURTH GRADE

When Jenni of the "I hate words" was assigned to my class, her mother came to me and said, "Jenni is afraid to be in a class with a man teacher." I did not know how to respond. I am a big person with a moustache, and I've been told that I can look a little scary. I assured Jenni's mother that I would move Jenni to the other fourth grade class if things did not work out. In my mind, I resolved to be so friendly and understanding that I would win her over. However, I was not prepared for how threatening I must really have appeared to Jenni.

At first, she would not look at me. She kept her eyes averted all through rugtime and the story I read to the class. When I showed the class where supplies were and while we made up the class rules, Jenni never looked directly at me. When I spoke to her, she trembled. I began to wonder if she would be able to stay in my class long enough for me to even try to put her at ease. When it came time for silent sustained reading, I asked her what she liked to read about.

"Horses," she whispered, looking away.

"There is a good horse book on the shelf," I said, "would you like to see it?" She nodded, and I went to get a picture book about horses. She ducked her head when I handed it to her and crept into a corner with a pillow to read. After a while, I noticed that she was turning the pages aimlessly.

I sat on the floor beside her and asked her to read me a little of it. She looked at me with dread and then looked helplessly at the book.

"The . . .", she started.

"Cart horse . . .", I prompted

". . . is a . . .", she continued.

". . . large . . .", I prompted.

The next word was 'horse', which she had just read, so I waited to see if she would pick it up. Instead, she just lowered her head and began to cry. Tears splashed, and shoulders heaved. I put my arm around her, and we sat there. I really didn't know what to do so I just tried something. I said, "Jenni, I've been thinking about what it would be like to be blind. How do you think we would be able to explain the color yellow to a blind person? Do you think we could do it so that a person who had always been blind could understand it?"

She looked up. "No," she said hesitantly.

I went on, relentlessly, wondering if I was making sense. "I don't think so either. I don't think anyone can be expected to know what they don't know. You are kind of like that, you know." I waited.

In a minute, her head came up a little. "How?"

"Well, you can't read very well, can you? And that is sort of like a kind of blindness. You are sort of blind to print. But you are a lot better off than someone who is really, truly blind." Again, I waited.

After a while, she said, "I am?" so softly that I almost didn't hear.

"Sure, a blind person is stuck with being blind, but you aren't stuck at all. In fact, you are going to learn to read this year." For just a moment, she thought I had some miracle up my sleeve. But now she saw it was just another one of those mind games that adults play. Her little face screwed back up, and she began to cry again. Jenni could see that this year was going to be as thoroughly wretched as the rest.

Ever hopeful, I tried another tack. "Jenni, I am not going to ask you to read at all for a while," I said. "Either I or another student will do all your reading for you. There's no point in making you more unhappy. In fact, school would be pretty okay for you if reading wasn't part of the deal, wouldn't it?" She did lift her head this time. She gazed at me as if I had just released her from prison.

"And we'll start right now," I said, "Go get two or three other horse books off the shelf, and we will read them in the hall." She scrambled to get the books, while I made a note of what I had just learned about her so I could start making a plan for Jenni.

I never did tell Jenni how I thought she would learn to read. However, I made sure that if another student or I weren't reading to her, then she was drawing a picture about something she had read with us. I also insisted she write every day, though in the beginning I had to script what she said. Her "writing", whether for her journal or to caption some drawing, typically consisted of four or five random letters, left to right. She had spaces between four or five "words" on each line.

Jenni was the oldest child I had ever taught who still wrote random strings of letters. It was the other side of the coin in terms of her literacy. Since she could not "hear" or identify phoneme segments, she could not use beginning sounds to attempt invented spellings. And she had been in a phonics drill program in her other school. Jenni had lots of oral language and concepts, lots of prior knowledge about the world and about stories—all the preliminary information that children need to become literate, but she couldn't access it.

Progress was slow. Jenni was read to, then she was read with, every day for the first three months of school, and we talked about reading. She wrote every day, and she drew pictures of what she had "read". I made sure that she worked with other girls who were also less than proficient readers, and the other girls delighted in being able to help each other.

Jenni began to develop some confidence. By November, I heard her laugh aloud for the first time. And on another day shortly thereafter, she became furious at Kent and shouted at him. While I was talking to them about controlling tempers, I realized that this new-found gumption was a sign of Jenni's increasing sense of competence in the world in general.

The two big breaks came together for Jenni. She and Lisa came up to me one day with secret smiles. Lisa said, "Jenni has something to show you, Mr. Bertrand."

Jenni opened an easy book on horses and began to read, accurately and without hesitation. The rest of the kids stopped what they were doing and listened. Jenni finished the book and stood there with her face shinning. We all started clapping. She was so proud. She had only memorized the book, but it was a tremendous step for her. Not only had she applied herself to a difficult task over a period of time (with her friend helping and encouraging her every day), but she had overcome the fear of failure that she associated with reading. She had figured out one strategy for handling print, and she had stepped from utter helplessness to making a book her own.

After that, progress was more swift. She began to try to learn to read, devising her own way into literacy with help from me and the teaching aide. She would get someone to read her a book a number of times. Often, when I read to her, she would be getting the fifth or tenth rendition of the book from the third or fourth person. Then, she would withdraw, and I would see her reading it to herself in a corner of the room. She was practicing. After a while, she would come to me and read the book to me in exchange for extravagant praise. After several of these occasions, I stopped her mother one day at pickup time and had Jenni read a book to her. She was overjoyed. Jenni was teaching herself to read through a novice/expert strategy. She was now also willing to practice.

As she began to acquire a larger sight vocabulary and also a few strategies for identifying unknown words, her writing improved as well. The first difference I noticed was that she was attempting initial letter sounds for the words she wrote in her journal. In addition, she began to correctly spell a few high frequency two and three letter words. Her journal began to take on the appearance of conventional writing with words of different lengths. She began to attempt syntactical conventions and used periods, capital letters when she remembered, and even commas. Her second breakthrough came when she wrote (with some help from a friend) a science report, revised and recopied it, and proudly displayed it on the poster she drew to illustrate and accompany it.

By the end of the school year, Jenni was reading and writing. She was still below grade level, but a sort of miracle had occurred. For the first time in her life, she was able to be independent, and she knew she was making progress. In general, Jenni had finally embarked on the journey into school learning and the power that bestows.

What characterizes all these children is that they had made little or no progress in school until they entered an integrated, literature based class. In direct-teaching classes, the only way for a child to master the task is the teacher's way. This is fine for simple things. But for complex, integrated skills like learning to read and write, the teacher's single way into the tasks fits few learning disabled children. If phonics and directed reading lessons are all a teacher has to offer, then few special children will learn much about literacy at all.

These three children do not represent all the types of "disabilities" from which children can suffer. However, these learning problems are typical, both in type and severity among the children. And though they differ in specifics, these students are more alike in the ways that count. None of them fit the concept of "grade level". No matter what their other skills and talents, no matter how intelligent, charming, creative, witty, or resourceful they were as individual people, they had been doomed to failure when they arrived at school.

Too many attempted remedies and special programs focus on what these children can't do. They "diagnose" weaknesses and "prescribe" as if the children are sick. Typically, the "remedy" consists of more of the same type of instruction that didn't succeed the first time, simplified and dumbed down. In other words, many of these children are instructionally disabled rather than learning disabled (Lyons, 1991). Outside of school, most children, like Davy and Kent, are excellent learners and problem solvers. Like all human beings, they have a strong drive to learn, to succeed, and to solve their own problems.

Too often, schools merely test and label but fail to offer LD and ADHD children a program in which it is possible to succeed (Weaver, 1994). Traditional schools are often very hard on children when they cannot meet the set of predetermined expectations known as "grade level" (Stice, Bertrand, & Bertrand,

1995). The deficit model for children which assumes, for example, that at-risk and learning disabled children need a reduced, restricted curriculum and a program based on hierarchical notions of learning and language development, is a major part of the problem. As I discovered time and again, these children learn just fine under the right conditions (Flores, Cousin, & Diaz, 1991).

My children needed the hope that, with hard work, success was possible. This is a feeling that they never had before. They needed emotional safety, the feeling that they could become smart, competent people. And they needed to believe that school was not a rigged deal against them, that the teacher was on their side. These feelings are intangible, but they come when a classroom is clearly structured so that the children can believe what you say and learn to trust—first you as the teacher and then themselves as learners.

References

Dudley-Marling, C. (1990). *When school is a struggle*. Richmond Hill, Ont.: Scholastic-TAB.

Flores, B., Cousin, P., & Diaz, E. (1991). Transforming deficit myths about learning, language and culture. *Language Arts*. (68), 370-379.

Lyons, C. (1991). Helping a learning disabled child enter the literate world. In D. DeFord, C. Lyons, & G. Pinnell. (Eds.) *Bridges to literacy: Learning from reading recovery*. Portsmouth, NH: Heinemann.

Poplin, M. (1988). The reductionist fallacy in learning disabilities: Replicating the past by reducing the present. *Journal of learning disabilities*. (21), 389-400.

Rhodes, L., & Dudley-Marling, C. (1988). *Readers and writers with a difference: A holistic approach to teaching learning disabled and remedial students*. Portsmouth, NH: Heinemann.

Weaver, C. (1994). *Success at last! Helping students with AD(H)D achieve their potential*. Portsmouth, NH: Heinemann.

Chapter 6

"Hoa Means "Flower": Language, Learners, and Culture in an ESL Multi-Age Classroom

Kathy Miller

I do not speak a second language well. I speak and read Spanish a little, from two years of Spanish in high school and one year in college. I speak street Spanish, but I certainly do not speak educated Spanish. So when I was asked to teach ESL, I knew I wasn't qualified. I also knew that I really wanted to work with second language students. It has been a trial and error learning experience for me ever since. I have learned much more from the children, I think, than they have learned from me

Bouahome was one of my more challenging learning experiences. She is almost ten now and doing quite well, but that is a rather recent phenomenon. When she first came to me, she was just starting kindergarten. Although she was born in the United States, she spoke no English. Her parents are from Laos and speak Laotian exclusively at home. Bouahome wouldn't speak at all when she started school. She had a very difficult time, partly because of her early English language limitations, but also because she was quick to lose her temper and easily frustrated. For years this combination kept her in trouble with her teachers and in turmoil with her parents and her peers.

My classroom is in a small annex behind the main school building. The room is large and lined with tall windows all along one length of the building. There are racks and shelves containing hundreds of books. Pens, pencils, markers and crayons fill the plastic buckets that dot the seating area, along with stacks of paper in the open cupboard in one corner. Tables accommodate the children, providing them ample work space for writing, art and other projects. The room even has a stove and small kitchen area, a make-believe dress up corner, and an area for book share and oral story complete with the typical rug and large rocking chair.

The room is warm and colorful, inviting to both children and adults. But it wasn't always that way. I remember when I first saw this annexed classroom. All it contained was a few tables and chairs, one teacher's desk, and a set of empty, dusty bookshelves. Now, resources that support language development and learning are everywhere. Children's work is displayed on the bulletin boards and windows, while much of it hangs from clotheslines stretched across the back of the room. Finished projects sit on shelves and on the floor along the one windowless wall. The room is full to overflowing with books, magazines, newspapers, posters, and other print sources. It is the first classroom in the school for children who are learning English as their second (or in some cases third) language. Like Bouahome, both the classroom and the program it houses have come a long way.

Although Bouahome learned to speak English fairly quickly, she had greater difficulty in math and in learning to read, and she was her own worst enemy. Once, when she received a grade of "F" in math in her regular classroom, she decided to stop doing any homework or taking any tests. She seemed to think she could punish the teacher for giving her a bad grade if she refused to cooperate. Her parents punished her severely. Finally, through intervention between home and the classroom teacher, we were able to get Bouahome to resume working in math.

Her family restricted their children to watching only educational television; consequently, Bouahome knew a great deal about science and geography. She had an excellent vocabulary and understood everything occurring in school. She was a very sophisticated and street-wise child who also understood what was taking place in her life outside of school. She could problem solve, think critically, and was an excellent learner. However, Bouahome applied these abilities to school learning on a selective basis.

Her favorite story was *Angel Child, Dragon Child* by Surat. She has loved that book since she was introduced to it in second grade. She has the text completely memorized, in fact, and has written several stories that are spin-offs of that book. She loved it so much that I gave her a copy so she would always have one of her own. Bouahome's love for that book sparked an entire series of letter writing to friends and family members "back home".

Although Bouahome still reads some picture books, she prefers chapter books now and reads two or three a week. She says all she wants to do is read. She especially likes *The Star Fisher* and *Dragonwings* by Yep. Asian students in the United States can relate to the problems and difficulties presented in both books as they try to function in two vastly different cultures. Bouahome has learned from reading books like these that other children experience some of the same difficulties she faces. These books have opened avenues and opportunities for dialogue between Bouahome and her fellow ESL students about ways to better handle their problems and the prejudices they encounter.

Her writings reflect the lessons she is learning from the literature she reads and the discussions in which she engages. Often, she writes notes about things she wants and needs to talk about. She also teaches me about Southeast Asian peoples. Bouahome is very pleased to be part of this chapter. She knows that I respect her, and she knows she is empowered to speak up in my classroom. Bouahome says she hopes other teachers will learn that the life of a refugee family is not always easy. It can be frightening and extremely difficult. She tells me it is hard to be poor in the United States.

Bouahome tested out of the ESL program at the end of her third grade year but continued to come to my classroom anyway. The other teachers agreed that the continued support of the ESL program was one of the few really positive events in her school life. Her other teachers say that when Bouahome spends even a few minutes with me in the morning before school starts, she is in a better mood for the rest of the day. She is less fidgety and better able to concentrate on her studies. Since she is a naturally loud child and has difficulty controlling her temper, conflict resolution techniques have given her some of the tools she needs to get along with her peers and teachers. She arrived early every morning, and as we talked, she helped me set up for the day. Bouahome continued to do this until she moved on into the new middle school.

Before she tested out of second language support, she participated successfully in all the activities and projects in the ESL classroom. She cooked, conducted science experiments, engaged in role-plays, demonstrated aspects of her culture, told and wrote stories, participated in shared book and readers theater, and engaged in many other language and literature based events. She also read from a wide variety of books.

Bouahome still comes to visit me and writes to me regularly, so I am able to keep up with some of her interests and much of her school work. I try to provide her with good books that we then talk about together. One book Bouahome especially liked was *The Secret Garden*, by Burnett. She asked me dozens of questions about India and the Indian terms and references in the story. She also read Babbitt's *Tuck Everlasting*, and Dahl's *James and the Giant Peach*. She becomes very involved in every book she reads if she likes the book, typically fantasizing about herself as the main character. Her writing nearly always reflects what she is reading. For example, in response to the story *Angle Child, Dragon Child*, she wrote:

> *Journal entry excerpt—November, 1993:*
>
> *In Vietnam the family name come first. In the legend of Vietnam, they descend from Angel Fairy and Dragon King. People call Vietnam Small Dragon and above it is a country called China. People call China the Great Dragon. Ut left her country called Vietnam to come to America. But she is still Vietnamese and she still had her Vietnamese name, Nguyen Hoa. Family is very important to Vietnamese. The name Hoa means flower . . .*

Family, name, and cultural identity are very important to Bouahome, too. She needs to preserve her language and cultural identity.

While Bouahome is definitely her own person, she is not an easy child to work with. She likes a book better when she picks it out than if someone else suggests a title. When she was just starting to read chapter books on her own, I suggested she read *Old Yeller* because I knew she liked animals. She was also fascinated by stories of pioneers or stories set in the American "old west". But, Bouahome did not like *Old Yeller* and told me that calling a dog a color name and then mispronouncing it was stupid. When I suggested she try it again in a year or two, she threw the book down and stormed out of the classroom. I don't suggest books anymore, but I continue to ask her what she is reading and what she thinks about it.

As Bouahome becomes really engrossed in a story, she tries to dramatize it with her friends. She tells them what to say and do as they act out stories both in class and out in the school yard. She makes up other stories for some of the main characters and "becomes" her favorite characters for a time. She thinks about story lines and characters and writes about them in her journal. I can just see her in Hollywood writing marvelous screen plays one day.

While many of her journal entries deal with the book she is currently reading, they also show how Bouahome works out personal problems.

Journal entry excerpt—April, 1994

Sometimes I feel like Emily in a book called The Star Fisher. *At her school [people] called her names and make fun of her when she talked Chinese. The same thing happens to me at school. When people make fun of my language and the way Laotians [do] I get mad. I tell them off. I get in trouble with teachers. It is not fair because they don't know the reasons for my yelling. I just try to remind myself about how Emily suffered from being different. Reading helps me think of new ways to stop people being prejudice.*

I'm glad I did not have a child as difficult and challenging as Bouahome when I first started teaching. That year, I taught in a Chapter I program in Texas, and I had several Hispanic children in my classroom. We had no bilingual or ESL curriculum and few materials. The school system expected the Spanish speaking children to score as well on the achievement tests as native English speaking children with no special assistance. If they didn't do as well, that was just too bad. I taught there for two years and then asked for a first grade. I knew my husband and I were moving back to Tennessee eventually, and I wanted to request first grade when we got back here. So I thought it would be a good idea to try it. I had a chance to teach in first grade for two years, and I took it. I thought I knew how to teach beginning reading. What was I thinking? I really became aware of the unfairness of English only when I taught those first graders.

That first year in first grade I had a Chinese student who neither spoke nor understood any English at the beginning of the year, and I didn't know what to do to help her. It was all just hit or miss, trial and error. I also had one Mexican American child who didn't learn to read. I was a very traditional teacher and spent a lot time on phonics skills and preset comprehension questions. We read the basal the way the teacher's manual suggested, one story per week, complete with seatwork, round robin oral reading, introducing the new words in advance . . . you know the drill. I knew it was boring even though most of the children seemed to learn fairly well, but I wanted to be a better teacher than that. I wanted to do more than just what the textbooks told me to do. I didn't know then that my conflict was due to the fact that what I had been taught to do and what I really wanted to do as a teacher reflected two contrasting views about language, learning, teaching, and the nature of learners.

What I *did* know was that I did not like the fact that at least one of my non-native speaking children wasn't learning to read. *Jose* spoke very little English and was small for his age, making me want to keep him in first grade for another year. I knew I should do something else to help him but I didn't know exactly what. Neither did anyone else in my school. His parents objected to my retaining him, and we soon found out that we couldn't hold him back just because he didn't have enough English. That year, the state required this school system to institute an ESL program. They sent me to a three day ESL workshop during the summer, and I became the ESL Director the last year I taught in that system. My total experience was having a few second language students and one 3 day inservice—it was absurd!

I knew I didn't really know anything about ESL, so when we moved to Tennessee I applied for a first grade position. However, when the director of special projects saw that I had ESL experience and had been in charge of an ESL program, she immediately wanted me to take an ESL position. I explained my situation to her, but the school system was desperate for teachers with *any* ESL experience. Large numbers of non-English speaking children were entering school, and the teachers were unprepared. Reluctantly, I agreed to teach ESL and help my new school system comply with the law. I also agreed to seek ESL certification as quickly as possible. I have been privileged to teach in the ESL program for more than fifteen years now.

Since I really didn't know what I was doing when I started, I had to figure out a lot of things on my own. I knew from personal experience and from my own attempts to learn Spanish that the old grammar translations for foreign language learning were totally unacceptable. I also knew that the audio-lingual, listen and memorize approach didn't work either. Certainly, teaching phonics skills to children who not only speak several different languages but who have heard very little English makes no sense. I also knew that they would be bored and their time squandered if I used meaningless workbooks, flashcards, and drills.

Figuring out what didn't work was the easy part, but I was still left with trying to figure out what would work. I asked myself what I believed about learning a second language. I realized that kids need to *use* their newly developing language. I knew they needed to see and hear what the language meant as they learned it, and they needed to do things with each other in their new language as they were learning it. I knew they needed to be read to. I believed they needed to write. Then I began to think about when my daughter was learning to talk and to read.

After teaching in Texas and before teaching in Tennessee, I had my daughter. The years I stayed home and raised my baby provided the data I used to reflect on what I knew, what I didn't know, and what kind of teacher I wanted to be. I thought about how she was beginning to read at four; how I had read dozens of books to her every month, practically from the day she was born. I remembered how she listened to me read and how we played with books and print from the time she was only a few months old. I knew what I'd done instinctively to help my daughter. When we went shopping, we wrote out our "lists". We "read" labels in stores. We cooked together, and she "read" the recipes. I began to see that I'd probably learned more about being a teacher from being a mother than from most of my college courses combined. I decided to set up my ESL classroom like a highly literate home where children are nurtured into reading and writing as a natural part of daily parent-child work and play in a warm and caring environment.

Armed with those understandings, goals and experiences, I also decided to learn as much as I could about what the experts say about teaching children to speak, read, and write a second language. When I took the ESL position in Tennessee, I knew that I wanted my students to become real readers and writers, not just to do well on tests. I wanted them to have the opportunity to become the kinds of readers and writers who love books and are highly successful in school. I also wanted the children to know that I respected and cared about their native languages and cultures and had no desire to repress them.

I began collecting materials I thought supported my developing instructional philosophy that reading and writing support literacy development when taught together, not separately. Today, we have over four thousand different children's books in this classroom. I always read aloud to my students, and I encourage them to read along. I also encourage them to write.

Children need to write every day. The choices are totally theirs, and I incorporate student generated writing projects into all aspects of my curriculum.

The reading experiences the children have are varied and involve silent reading, reading in pairs and small groups, and some whole group reading. They read books and stories of their own choosing. Sometimes, they read to find information or as a model for their writing and their own bookmaking. Their reading is always purposeful.

We also engage in other literacy based activities developed by the children. We act out favorite stories and fairy tales. We make simple costumes and scenery for our own productions. *The Napping House* by Wood is a favorite dramatization in my room, as is *Lon Po Po* by Ed Young. Other literacy activities revolve around local events in the newspaper. Once we started a school clean-up campaign that originated from a newspaper article one of the children brought in about conditions on local school grounds. Several of my classes became involved in a recycling campaign because of a discussion that ensued following the reading of another article in the newspaper. The children made posters and gathered information. They found out where to dispose of aluminum cans. They worked to collect the cans, and we made quite a nice little profit on the project which we spent on books of their choosing for the classroom.

Since I also wanted my classroom to reflect a highly literate family atmosphere, I looked for things to do with my students that were natural ways families use literacy. We write lists, cook together, shop, bank, and read and write about places and events on field trips. In addition to reading to them every day and writing to them, having them write to me and to each other and writing in their journals, we do many other things that involve reading and writing in the world. We set up classroom stores and businesses and created venues for authentic language use. We've had a grocery store, a travel agency, an airline terminal, a post office, and a veterinary clinic in our classroom.

Right now we have a bakery in the room and are reading about all the ways bread is made and used throughout the world. That has been fascinating, and the children have supplied much of the information. We have learned about bread in each of their native cultures. The bakery idea came from reading the book *Bread, Bread, Bread* by Morris. The children gathered recipes for various kinds of bread baked and eaten around the world. Indian fry bread, a native American bread, is one of their favorites. They have brought in bread and bread recipes from their native countries. They have read the recipes, planned trips to the store, and calculated costs of baking various types of bread. They have baked many different types of breads and advertised their baked goods with posters, flyers, and ads in the class newspaper. They have prepared their own menus, written their own recipes, written stories and information pieces about bread, and sold their wares to other students.

Because so many of the children come from homes where their families grow a vegetable garden, we are going to operate a fruit and vegetable stand this spring. This will require writing to advertise, as well as math to figure out what things should cost, how to make change, and how to determine our profit. We are also going to experiment with freezing and canning vegetables as our science project. That will require some reading to know how to process the food and writing so we can label our products and document what we think will happen compared to what really does happen. I plan to have the class participate in planting our own garden in back of the building. Several of the children thought up that idea, and I rather like it.

I have come to love what I do and to believe in it thoroughly. My students do very well on achievement tests, but beyond that they like to come to school and feel good about themselves as learners. That is the important part. It means they have a better chance to keep on growing as learners when they leave me. But teaching the way I do is not a magic cure. Students still struggle, and I still have problems.

Two children come to mind immediately when I think of students who have caused me sleepless nights. They are very different from each other, but together they represent the wide range of abilities, backgrounds, needs and strengths I encounter each day in this classroom. One child doesn't really need me at all now, while the other may be allowed to stay with me until he moves on to middle school.

Pedro came to me in October two years ago. Seven years old, he was placed in first grade and in my ESL classroom. He could not read his own name and spoke no English. However, he understood some of what was said to him in English. Pedro and his older brother are the only members of their immediate family, except for one grandfather, who have ever been to school. In fact, the grandfather, who is the only educated relative Pedro has, owns several restaurants and is doing quite well. Pedro's family came to the States from Mexico to work in one of the restaurants owned by the grandfather and operated by cousins. Neither Pedro's mother nor his father read or write Spanish, and they speak very little English.

Life is difficult for Pedro and his family. They are very poor. They all work in the restaurant, even little Pedro helps out after school. The hope is that one day perhaps Pedro and/or his brother will be able to manage or own their own business. Pedro also has a twisted leg and a pronounced limp. Efforts are underway to help him have corrective surgery through the Shriners. Right now he wears a brace that twists his leg straight. It is very painful and causes him to have problems concentrating in school. I do not think Pedro realizes how brave he is. The other ESL children like him very much and try to protect him.

Pedro is a high strung, nervous child. He is shy with the other children and easily embarrassed. When he first came to the school he had so little English that he couldn't even ask to go to the bathroom. I was told that he was very likely a slow learner, but I don't pay much attention to pronouncements like that made on such limited information. Pedro was placed in the ESL classroom for one period, and in the regular classroom for the rest of the school day. The principal that year didn't really understand the needs of a school with a large ESL population. He did not allow me to suggest which classrooms might be best for the non-English speaking children. As a result, Pedro was placed in a classroom with a teacher who had little experience with ESL children. She didn't know how to help him, and she didn't want help herself. Pedro had a very difficult and unhappy first year. He finished the year hating reading and refusing to write.

Even though he read very little and didn't write, he had actually made some progress. By the beginning of second grade, he understood nearly everything that was said to him and could speak understandable English. Nevertheless, his self-image was still pretty low. Perhaps the most significant problem was the fact that Pedro had not been read to in his first grade classroom. Although he was read to daily in the ESL classroom, he could not follow a story line. He couldn't retell a story. He couldn't even point to "who did what" or match word labels for familiar objects. In fact, at the beginning of second grade he still did not know that print in English and Spanish moves from left to right, nor had he developed much voice print match. That is, he couldn't use a pointer even with a very easy big book that he had memorized. I suspected that Pedro hadn't understood what print was when he started first grade, and he finished the year with still very little idea of what words are and what they do. He said he couldn't read because he was not Lao, the national origin of the majority of his classmates.

Since none of Pedro's family read or write, the only print he sees his family use are labels on cans and other grocery items and menus from the restaurant. I spend a lot of time examining and using menus with the children. Today, two years later, Pedro reads, writes and helps me teach newly arrived children. Since the students have a bakery in the classroom right now, Pedro is reading everything connected with bakeries. He knows how much every item costs and where to find the price. He reads recipes for donuts, muffins, and sourdough bread. He can calculate how much a dozen will cost, make change, and write his own recipe or make up his own menu. He likes to draw, then write captions and labels, and he draws very well. But initially, he produced letter-like shapes that did not represent speech.

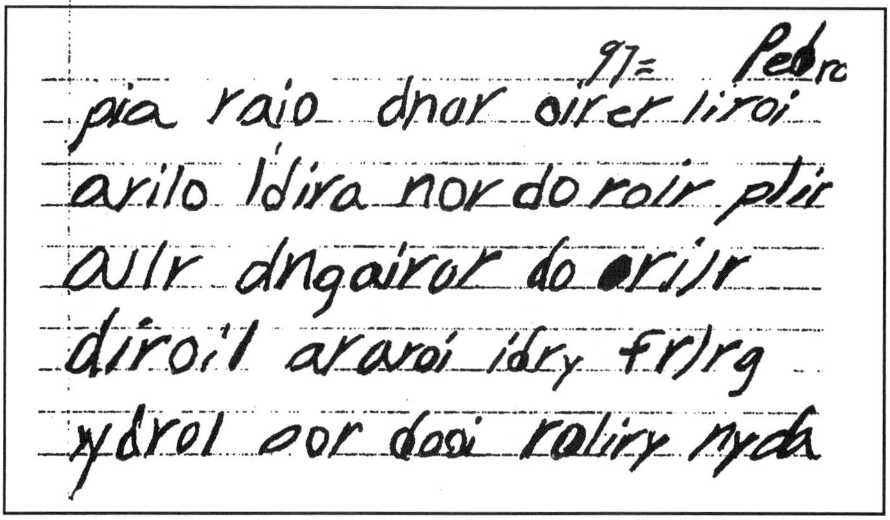

Figure 6.1 Pedro's Writing Sample #1

His writing development has approximated the stages younger children go through. Pedro's greatest strength is that he has a good ear for speech sounds. He can always tell what sound is at the beginning of a word, and he pays attention to letters for beginning and ending sounds in words he wants to write. The realization that he could write words someone else could read by using the initial letter-sounds he was learning was a big breakthrough for Pedro early in second grade. After that, his writing and his reading just took off. He knew what he wanted to say and was willing to take risks with spelling and writing. His writing began to show a sense of sentence. He always used capitals at the beginning and end punctuation to conclude sentences.

Now, he writes anything most any other child his age in fourth grade can write. He writes his own stories, pen pal letters, and information books. His first draft writing is sloppy, partly because that is just the way Pedro is and partly because writing is still not all that easy for him. There is always a lot of revising and editing going on with Pedro's stories and letters, but he has really wonderful ideas. Frequently, his stories are quite long and involved. Now, when we discuss a piece of writing, he can tell me in great detail about each character or event. He has well developed story lines and writes in a variety of genres and for a wide variety of audiences. This is hardly the progress of a slow learner.

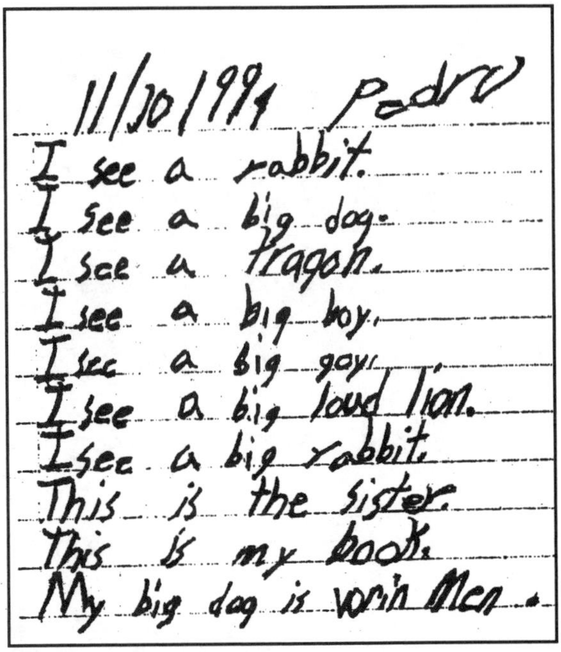

Figure 6. 2   Pedro's Writing Sample #2

By the end of second grade, Pedro was very self-directed. He was purposefully trying to improve his reading and writing. He was well aware of the fact that he was still the only second grader who came to ESL with the first graders. He carried a dictionary with him and looked up words he needed to spell or for which he wanted a meaning. Often, he would write a sentence using words he was trying to learn. That was a teaching idea he learned from his regular second grade teacher.

Pedro really blossomed. At some point, it all just came together for him. Now he knows what is happening and that he is part of it. His writing shows learning in science and social studies. His regular classroom teachers say he is reading grade and age appropriate material with fluency and understanding. Pedro says he likes to read storybooks now because "that's easy". He can retell any story he reads and, like all good learners his age, asks questions about all sorts of things from why bread rises to what happened to the dinosaurs. In fact, he takes books home every night and reads instead of watching television. He reads any story about animals he can find. He has recently been reading fairy tales that were read to him when he couldn't read and probably couldn't understand the English. He self-corrects and relates what he is reading to his own experiences. He employs the same strategies other proficient readers use.

This week Pedro saw me copying some pages out of his journal. He wanted to know why I was copying his journal. I told him that he had learned to write so well I was thinking of using some of his writing in a book if it was all right with him and his parents. Pedro was surprised. Then he said, "If you are going to use my writing in a book, I want it all to look like I can write now." He wanted me to let him correct everything. We talked about the fact that if he went back and corrected everything no one would be able to tell how much he had learned. Finally, he agreed to leave the old writing the way it was. He was actually quite proud of himself, and I am proud of Pedro, too.

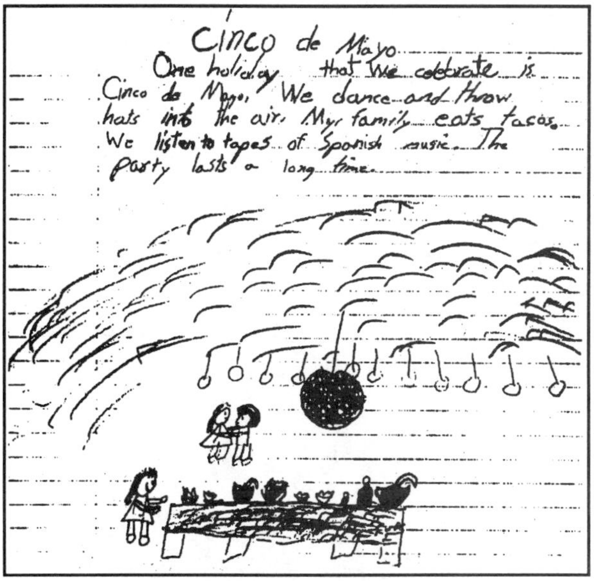

Figure 6.3 Pedro's Writing Sample #3

While most children need some time and support as they add the second language to their linguistic repertoire, this is especially true if the second language is spoken and heard only at school. *Kason* is a good example of what it's like for most children with limited English. She is Laotian. Her family speaks a little English. They want to learn English because they are becoming citizens and plan to stay here and make this their home. But the family is stressed financially. The parents and her siblings all work. One parent works days and one works nights, so that some adult is in the house with the children at all times. Unfortunately, that parent is usually sleeping while the other is gone so Kason is frequently left alone. Kason has been with me for two years now and has made remarkable progress. She has gone through all the phases that you'd expect—from emergent literacy to more fluent and independent levels.

She has learned English from the children she plays with and the teenaged babysitter who lives down the street who stays with her at night on the weekend. Kason is very verbal. She has a large vocabulary and appears to learn by memorizing. She doesn't forget anything she hears or reads. She is not very good at sounding out English words, but she can use initial letter sounds to help her identify unfamiliar words as she reads.

Kason's best friend is Amy. Amy helps Kason learn. Whatever Amy does, Kason follows suit. If Amy writes about a dragon, so does Kason. If Amy draws a picture of a rainbow, Kason does too. If Amy wants to read a certain book, Kason must read it. If I receive a "love note" from Amy, Kason sends one immediately.

Figure 6.4   A Note from Kason

You'd think they were twins if you looked at their work for the day. In some instinctive way, Kason knew it was a good idea to apprentice herself to Amy, and it is working. Amy is one of the reasons Kason is becoming such a good reader. Amy plays school with Kason. Of course, Amy is the teacher. They use books from my room and sometimes play school outside the classroom door after school. I hear Amy explaining to Kason in a very teacher-like voice just what to do and how to do it. Amy reads with Kason, and together they have read aloud and discussed many books Amy already knew how to read. Kason reads just like Amy, with her inflections and pronunciation. Talk about engagement, demonstrations, approximation, and immersion!

Like many of the other children, Kason likes to sketch along with her writing. She also likes information books almost better than storybooks right now. This past week we read *The Egg* by Jeunesse and deBourgoing. Kason was fascinated with the idea that dragonflies and ladybugs lay tiny eggs. We spent a few days reading books about ladybugs several weeks ago because there were so many of them in the environment. She found out that most insects lay eggs and wondered why "birds and bugs both lay eggs." After we read the egg book, Kason wanted to make a book in the shape of an egg with all sorts of facts about eggs. It turned out well.

Figure 6.5   Kason's Book, *The Egg*

Like most of the children who come to my classroom, Kason does fine on achievement tests. She may not be in the ninety-ninth percentile, but Kason scores in the average ranges, higher than many of the native English speaking children in her regular classroom. She can read without Amy, and she writes at least as well as she can speak. Even though her English vocabulary is still limited and unfamiliar terms give her difficulty, she has this classroom with all its books and hands-on learning. Kason will not be in the ESL classroom next year, but I will keep in touch with her until she goes on to middle school.

For me, teaching ought to be embedded as much as possible in authentic social contexts. Language in all its forms is the primary tool for learning and sharing. I use the same instructional strategies and approaches many regular, learner-centered teachers might employ. I read aloud to the children daily and I create guided reading lessons and other focus lessons as the children need them. I use dictated group stories, daily writing, and opportunities for real life reading, writing, math, science, and social studies experiences.

One of my students' favorite learning activities is making big books for the classroom. We make several different kinds of big books each year. One year several students decided to turn *Brown Bear, Brown Bear*, by Martin into an enlarged accordion book using matte board. When completed, the book stood alone and stretched across the room. The students took it to all the kindergarten and first grade classes and read it with the children. This past year we used a camera and took photos of interesting people around the school. The students interviewed each person whose photo was selected and then wrote a story about the person. Many of the people photographed were other second language students. Their stories were revised, edited and bound into a class big book that all the students love to read and reread. As Heath and Magnolia (1991) suggest, instructional events should build on the world and on the linguistic knowledge base second language learners bring to the classroom.

I know that language learning happens best when children are immersed in it, through talking, hearing and seeing good literature and encountering a wide variety of information. It does not occur linearly in a lock-step, sequential skills manner. I know that the children require many demonstrations of how language works. They need a risk-free, cooperative, learner-centered environment. They need rich content to explore and a multitude of learning events in which to engage. I listen to and observe what the children are interested in and want to do. Then I try to find a way to incorporate that into the curriculum (Goodman, 1985).

Sometimes students from diverse cultures and language groups think that they must choose between being successful in school and being true to who they are—to their own culture (Au, 1993). I do not want that to happen to my students. Celebrating each student's language and cultural heritage is one of the ways I try to support them. I also focus on their strengths and interests. I employ children's and adolescent literature that is reflective of diverse cultures and real situations and problems to which the students can relate. I talk to them about how to handle difficult situations, and I try in every way to show them that I regard them as knowledgeable and competent people.

Rigg and Allen (1989 p. viii), list at least five principles of good instruction in an ESL classroom or in a regular education classroom for that matter:

1. People who are learning another language are, first of all, people.
2. Learning a language means learning to do the things you want to do with people who speak that language.
3. A person's second language, like the first, develops globally, not linearly.
4. Language develops best in a variety of rich contexts.
5. Literacy is part of language, so writing and reading develop alongside speaking and listening.

These principles apply to classrooms with learners from diverse cultures and various languages. I hope that each of these principles is visible in my classroom. I believe the success my students achieve is unmistakably linked to the learner-centered, language and literature-based philosophy I have adopted and adapted in support of second language learners. I hope, too, that more teachers will choose to become ESL and bilingual educators and that they will receive the training they need.

References

Au, K. (1993). *Literacy instruction in multicultural settings*. New York: Holt, Rinehart & Winston.

Burnett, F. (1987). *The secret garden*. New York: Scholastic.

Dahl, R. (1961). *James and the giant peach*. New York: Puffin.

Gibson, F. (1956). *Old Yeller*. New York: Harper.

Goodman, Y.(1985).Kid-watching:Observing children in the classroom. In A. Jaggar & M. Smith-Burke. (Eds.), *Observing the language learner*. Newark, DE: IRA.

Heath, S., & Magnolia, L. (Eds.) (1991). *Children of promise: Literate activity in linguistically and culturally diverse classrooms.* Washington, DC: NEA.

Jeunesse, G., & de Bourgoing, P. (1989). *The egg.* New York:Scholastic.

Morris, A. (1989). *Bread, bread, bread.* New York: Scholastic.

Rigg, P., & Allen, V. (Eds.) (1989). *When they don't all speak English: Integrating the ESL student into the regular classroom.* Urbana, IL: NCTE.

Surat, M. (1983). *Angel child, dragon child.* New York: Scholastic.

Wood, D., & Wood, A. (1984). *The napping house.* San Diego, CA: Harcourt, Brace, Jovanovich.

Yep, L. (1975). *Dragonwings.* New York: Harper & Row.

Yep, L. 1991). *The star fisher.* New York: Scholastic.

Chapter 7

"Won't Nobody Come!"
Four Critical Components for
Creating Successful Parent/School
Partnerships in
Distressed Communities

John E. Bertrand

The issue of parent/school partnerships may seem a little out of place in a book where everything else is about young children at risk of school failure. However, parent enthusiasm and commitment to schooling is a major component of what fuels learner performance as well as what encourages, protects, and sustains good teachers.

Young learners respond most strongly to the expectations that are held for them, positive or negative. These expectations come from their parents along with committed local teachers and school leaders and even the larger social group. Exemplary programs for children at risk are developed from time to time, but they only serve a comparative few and frequently disappear after a while under the weight of bureaucratic pressure and political incursions into classrooms.

While each locale is unique with its own set of limitations and attributes, there are principles that cut across the specifics of place. They may not be known in advance by those who seek to help schools, especially in low-income or otherwise beleaguered communities, but they are often discerned by the parents themselves out of necessity as they attempt to create something that works. The two highly successful parent/school partnership programs I was privileged to know first hand have taught me what is possible in places I thought no such entity could exist, much less flourish. These programs have dramatically changed schooling in each of their distressed but determined communities. From them we may derive four basic principles which, if followed, help insure that nearly anyone can begin a successful parent/school partnership program.

In the following cases, the names and communities of the participants are disguised to protect privacy. However, you will probably agree that they could be almost anywhere in the U.S. The attributes that characterize distressed communities are not dependent on regional location. They derive from poverty, the politics of race, and from loss of hope and loss of community. One program is school-based in a integrated primary school. The other is community-based, involving a number of schools. These two cases come from a larger study of successful parent/school programs. They were selected because they exemplify the characteristics of successful programs and because they illustrate that successful programs can flourish even in the most distressed places.

Susan Black and the Maryhurst School

The Maryhurst community reached its zenith in the late 1860s, after the first modern bridge was built from the downtown area across the river. Large homes went up as affluence expanded. In its day, Maryhurst was a neighborhood of grand avenues, stately homes, and rich carriages. Over the years, as the city expanded, Maryhurst became less prestigious and more middle class. Homes were cut up into flats; apartment buildings were constructed; population increased. The passage of time saw a continued downward spiral in this community as the more affluent citizens expanded the city in other directions.

By the 1930s, Maryhurst was a mixed community of African and Anglo Americans, mostly poor. The transformation became complete just after World War II. The heart of the neighborhood, mostly decayed buildings, was razed, and enormous blocks of federally subsidized housing projects built. Over the ensuing decades, even these have decayed. Today, the neighborhood is known as Dodge City to the police and many of its inhabitants. Drugs are sold openly; murder on the streets is too common; the people are wary. The population is about 90% African-American, largely unemployed, and largely disengaged with mainstream society. A minority of the inhabitants finish ninth grade; fewer yet finish high school. To say the least, Maryhurst qualifies in all respects as a distressed inner-city community.

The school is a two-story, red brick structure of typical old Victorian-style that was the pride of every community in the country in the 1920s, 30s, 40s. This one is T-shaped. The long hall was built by the WPA in the early days of the Depression, and the crossbar followed just after the Second World War. It has acquired the smells, patina, and aura that inevitably accompany old school buildings with their high ceilings, large windows, tile floors and tracks of the thousands of students it has served over the decades.

Currently, the building hunkers at the edge of the projects. Before the ten-foot, chainlink fence was constructed around the grounds, each morning found the children's playground littered with broken glass, empty shell casings, syringes, and worse. Often the school windows were broken. Layabouts and unemployed teenagers hung out on the playground before the fence came and often harassed parents and teachers on their way into the building. When busing for purposes of desegregation became mandatory, many white citizens did not want their children brought into this neighborhood, and the school board closed the school.

It was resurrected a few months later when local money, combined with a federal grant, allowed it to be reopened as a neighborhood preschool/ kindergarten program, since busing did not apply to children below first grade. The staff, a black principal and seven white teachers, define their jobs as providing the first, best intervention into the lives of children who are extremely poor and who have few, if any, advantages. The program was kicked off with much publicity, but then the teachers, parents, principal, children, and community were left to work out the details on their own.

What followed was probably inevitable. Well-intentioned teachers did what they could to reach out to the community and were met with suspicion, distrust, and occasionally open hostility. The parents were people who had not been winners in the competitive, winners-and-losers atmosphere of their own schools. Many could not read very well. Most regarded the good intentions of the teachers as just another phony, supercilious program. The breaking point came when several of the teachers decided to start a school-community partnership program in the school. They sent notes home inviting parents to come to an organizational meeting one evening during the school week. Out of nearly 140 children who attended the school, a total of five parents came.

The teachers were outraged. They thought their good intentions were unappreciated and misunderstood. The parents, they thought, just did not care. Some of the teachers became disillusioned and began to make rather cynical comments. Others became resigned to doing the job without support from the school system or the community. The principal, caught between his responsibilities to the teachers and school system and the unrealistic expectations of many parents because of his race, found only frustration in trying to bring the light of empathy and understanding to either side.

And so it went. Each morning, the parents would emerge from the alleys and streets of the projects that bordered the school and walk their children across the playground to the parking lot. There, the teachers would be waiting to take the children into the school. Few words other than the bare civilities were exchanged. Teachers stayed on the school grounds, and parents did not come into the school unless summoned for an official meeting. The only thing these adults shared in common was their concern for the children; both sides were convinced that the other did not care, did not understand that they were ineffectual, misguided, and inappropriate.

This situation, which characterizes all too many high-risk schools, might have continued indefinitely if one other factor had not intervened. The state department of education offered seed money to start school-community partnership demonstration programs at twenty sites across the state. The principal and teachers at Maryhurst, after considerable soul searching, decided to apply for a grant and try one more time. They received enough money for a salary for one person and less than $2000 in operating expenses, but it was enough. They began the search for a person to fill the job of coordinator. The job description they used was indeterminate. They knew the outcomes they wanted, but they had little idea how to get there. After interviewing a number of well-intentioned people who shared their lack of ideas, they settled on and hired a primary grade teacher who had taught in a nearby school for the previous two years.

The problems Susan Black faced were prodigious: a distressed community, polarized teachers, hostile parents, and 50% of the children leaving kindergarten unable to qualify for first grade. But Susan had learned something in her time in the projects. She believed that the parents could be powerful allies, both in terms of influencing the life of the school and in influencing the school system to produce more of the things the school needed to prosper. She was not discouraged by the failure of the first parent club. She patiently set about to form a new one.

She thought parents would be interested in classes on parenting skills. With the money that accompanied her position, she bought a sequenced program of child stimulation and reading-to methods for parents. Now all she had to do was get the parents to come. She set about to overcome their suspicions and fears.

On registration day in August, Susan and several teachers staged a "parade" through the projects. In two pickup trucks, dressed as clowns, teachers played the piano, held up promotional signs, and gave out flyers. The van from a local radio station accompanied them, pumping out music and letting residents speak over the air. Crowds gathered wherever the trucks stopped, and the initial message was broadcast through the community in a way the insured that even those who did not attend heard about it. This was followed in the next few days by a barrage of notes home, flyers, and exhortations to the children. Susan stood every morning and evening in the "no-man's land" at the edge of the playground urging parents as they brought and picked up children to come to the first meeting and reminding them of the date and time.

She began a practice of home visits that she maintains to this day. Dodge City is not safe even for the residents, much less middle class women who do not know the turf. The mothers looked at her in wonder. Some were receptive; others were not. She was appalled at the condition of the projects. Broken windows, sagging floors, faulty wiring, broken plumbing . . . all these and more characterized the old and unmaintained buildings. At one house, the mother promised to come to the parent club meeting and then gazed at her with wide eyes. "Where you going next?" she inquired. "Let me walk with you there." It was the beginning of hundreds of miles walked in Dodge City. Today, everyone knows who Susan is. It is known in the projects that she does not volunteer things to the police. Even some of the known criminals speak to her, and she is "shouted" from block to block as she goes. She proudly says that she has never felt herself in danger on any of her home visits. But on that first day, years ago, she was not so sure.

"Won't nobody come," the custodian told her confidently, concerned that she was going to be disappointed when Susan asked him to set up 25 chairs in the second floor classroom designated as the Parent Program room. In preparing for that first parent organizing meeting the custodian indicated that ten chairs would be more than sufficient. At 10:00 that morning, 80 parents crowded into the room as Susan and the custodian scrambled to get more chairs in place. At this meeting, several parents spoke forcefully about problems in the community and supported the belief that they could all cope better if they were organized. They called the new organization the "Parents Club", and they decided to meet twice a week. Susan kept the meeting room open for anyone who wanted to drop in anytime during the school day. The large turnout continued. Between sixty and eighty parents a week came. Across the school year, 105 out of a possible 175 parents came and participated at various times, an astonishing number.

Susan did not use manuals or impose rules. The parents shared their expectations and fears. They wanted what all parents want, that their children should have safe, happy, productive lives. Their fears centered around crime, child abuse, adult illiteracy, and their inability to visit the schools their other children were bused to because not one in ten had a car. Some of them cried, and some raged. The club became first a place where one could speak without fear of ridicule or reprisal. Susan refereed when necessary, and they tried out a few ground rules: no ridiculing each other, and no using information learned in the club against anyone.

Susan attempted to structure the meetings around the materials, but there were so many needs that superseded parenting skills that she was soon swamped in individual requests for referrals to other agencies and offices. Some of the referrals were from the group. For instance, after a police community affairs person came to speak to the group, they requested and received additional patrol of their apartments during meeting times to prevent burglars from taking advantage of their predictable absences. It was clear to Susan from the start that some of her credibility would depend on her ability to locate resources. She brought in Human Services, the police, adult literacy programs, community dental service, and a hairdresser, to name only a few.

As things progressed, parents became more interested in parenting skills. They responded to the lessons more actively. As Susan's credibility increased, she influenced the members to begin to accept other ideas. She obtained children's literature and began a program wherein parents got to earn credit towards owning books by reading to their children. This, in turn, led to a great deal of informal, mutual help between parents who could read relatively well and those who could not. Many parents read a book to a child only after practicing it at the club the previous afternoon.

When cold weather came, many of the children lacked suitable clothing, winter shoes, socks, or boots. Susan began a drive to obtain second hand clothes and shoes from outside the community. These, along with clothes that parents themselves traded, began to make a difference. Susan's credibility and goodwill within the community increased accordingly. She continued home visits, counseled with parents, referred them to various resources and agencies, arranged transportation, and advised them on matters ranging from marriage to finances.

The parents began to use the Parents Club room as the focal point for their daytime social life. Susan was not there all the time as she conferred with social workers, made home visits, organized events, fund raised, and visited classrooms. Parents took over the running of the club more completely as time progressed. In the first year, Susan encouraged parents to participate in the booths the teachers set up at the fund-raising carnival. In the second year, the teachers set up the booths, but the parents operated them and looked after the money. When carnival time came near in the third year, she assigned the project to the Parents Club and left them to it. It was a highly successful endeavor.

Susan has worked in this community for several years now. She has learned the hard way that new parenting skills, as admirable as they may be, are of little avail if the general level of distress in the home is not lightened. Her own words explain this better than anyone.

> *You know that knowledge really is power. I sometimes feel like a one eyed person in the land of the blind. Stuff I just take so much for granted that I can't even remember where I learned it I've known it so long, since childhood, is just a mystery to most of the parents. Like reading a city map. We had a whole club meeting on how to find an address on a city map and then to figure out what bus to take to get there. But this is really important to the parents. It's no good to tell them to go get food stamps if they can't get there. And some of the kids come to school and you can see they haven't been fed properly. And when I visit it isn't that they are neglected; there just isn't any food in the house. Now they teach each other how to get around the city and they go together because they know each other from the Club and know they can trust each other.*

Resources became the focus from the first day. In that first year, the Parents Club had visitors and a presentation from the local dairy council, a mental health center, the police department on several occasions, the fire and rescue department, Parents Anonymous, the housing project social work department, the housing project security department, the local GED examination board, and a number of others. The school library became a place for parents to look up information, and the club room a place to practice and teach each other grammar and math in preparation for job exams and, in a few cases, the GED exam. For many, the Parents Club was a first experience with cooperation with peers in any meaningful or positive way.

Parents raised money for field trips, but for themselves at first rather than for the children. Susan recruited a local bank in the Adopt-a-School program and then used this entree' to obtain occasional use of the bank's van and driver. The club went to the bank and learned about using money in forms other than cash. They went to a good-quality, local restaurant for dinner. They went to a park for a picnic, and they visited a local nursing home. Everyone had her hair fixed at the local vocational-technical high school, and they toured the program in the process. They wrote thank-you letters everywhere they went. None of this is remarkable until one remembers that for many of these adults, these trips were their first experiences with facilities outside their community. The Parents Club, in providing cooperative, internally supportive, social confidence for parents, also gave many of them their first contacts with mainstream society.

The payoffs began in a short time. Parents began to volunteer to help on field trips for the children. They helped develop surveys that smoothed out departure problems at the end of the school day. At Thanksgiving, the club gave a brunch for the school faculty. At Christmas, the parents produced a play, using the services of a local little theater director who volunteered his time. They performed "Snow White and the Seven Dwarfs" for the children, using costumes and a set they made themselves. On Valentine's Day, forty parents went from classroom to classroom carrying posters and banners they had made promoting education and love. Each child got a puzzle and a card, made by parents. As the school became more and more important in their lives, their feelings were communicated to the children. Discipline problems with children became fewer and more quickly settled. Parent conferences showed more confidence on both sides. Children bragged to each other how many times one parent or another had attended club meetings. In the process, parents learned the importance of stimulation of young children and their exposure to language experiences. The basis of the program, parenting skills, continues to be the focus of what Susan does. She has become the fulcrum for how this school operates. Her problem solving abilities are exceptional; her ability to see all sides and either mediate or refer people to resources makes her indispensable to everyone. She radiates positive attitudes. She constantly invites people to meetings, to try new things, and to persevere. She is there for every occasion. Over the years, she has made over 2000 home visits, all on foot across the housing project. Everyone respects her.

In trying to summarize what Susan has accomplished, an observer is perplexed. Surely, Dodge City appears to be as miserable and distressed as ever. But change is real when four to five hundred families are affected for the better in ways nearly too numerous to count. The school is an infinitely more pleasant and productive place for children. The Parents Club is an ongoing institution which is now an ingrained part of the community. People, many of them teachers, who thought that positive change for the residents of Dodge City was impossible, were wrong. Children who otherwise would have inherited their parents' mistrust of schools and teachers are now performing on a higher level through first grade and beyond. For an observer who understands the community and its history, the changes are directly visible and extraordinary.

KAYE WHITE AND THE SNEAD COUNTY PARENT EDUCATION PROJECT

Snead County is at the other end of the state from Maryhurst and at the other end of the spectrum in several ways. It shares the problems faced by most rural, poor communities: isolation, nearly non-existent tax base, low levels of education and low educational standards among the inhabitants, and a permanently depressed economy. Snead Point, the county seat, consists of about twelve city blocks of commercial enterprises and mixed housing in the middle of 1200 square miles of hills, hollows, and back roads. There are about 6800 people in the county, of whom about 1400 are students in the county schools. There is only one main road through the county and steep ridges tower over the cars as they travel its banked curves, following the watercourse in the valley bottom.

There is not much agriculture in Snead County. The land is steep, and the soil rocky. Trailers and small homes cling to the ridgesides. On a patch near the river lies the only airfield for miles, a privately owned grass strip. Forests climb the mountains and ridges, and county roads, barely paved, snake over the passes, taking the lines of least resistance.

The county has been economically depressed as long as anyone can remember. As with many rural communities, natural resources are a large part of local income, in this case, timber. There are only three employers in the county with more than twenty employees, a table top factory, a furniture factory, and an electric motor factory. Unemployment habitually hovers around thirteen percent, roughly triple the national average. Employment at the furniture and electric motor factories remains fairly constant. Only a few new hires occur each year, and they are primarily from within the ranks of the families of present employees.

Snead County was the subject of a number of much publicized social engineering programs during the height of the Great Society days. Job training programs were started; an educational television station was built; and several new types of welfare were introduced. Today, not even the remnants of these programs can be deduced. Of the county's population, nearly half live beneath the poverty level, and 45% of the families receive welfare benefits of some sort. Ninety percent of the children are on the free lunch program in school.

There has been no new investment in the county for many years. Main Street boasts no fast food franchises; there is no movie theater. Kaye White, the local home/school partnership coordinator, attributes the failure of social engineering to the ignorance of well-intentioned outsiders who arrived with the "solutions" already in hand to local problems. To a great extent, she says, people were trained for jobs that did not exist within any reasonable driving distance, and programs carried a strong urban bias. Most locals had no desire or intention of moving.

The 1990 census found no non-white people in the county. Poverty, subsistence farming, timber cutting, the three corporate employers, and a few other jobs have characterized the economy of the county for decades. People think of the status quo as a necessary way of life, and there is little agitation for change. Expectations tend not to exceed reality, and few people leave the county permanently, as the stable population figures attest. There is a strong sense of family loyalty among these descendants of the original settlers. They have avoided the mobility, family break-ups, and divorce rates that plague much of the rest of the country; however, they appear to find it difficult to adjust to change.

In spite of that, a few changes are coming. The main highway is being widened. The county clerk said, "They're taking the whole top off of the mountain over on the county line to fix the road." It will remain a two-lane road, though. The county executive and the County Court have purchased 100 acres of land near Snead Point for an industrial park. They have "promises" from prospective employers, they say. Recently, when a new prison was proposed for the area, residents gathered in meetings and signed enough petitions to kill the idea. The prison was seen as a danger to traditional values, a threat to what locals viewed as best about their way of life.

Isolation most marks the lives of the inhabitants of these hills. It is a 45 mile drive over bad roads to the nearest town of any size, where there are movies, restaurants, shopping centers, and so on. Even television reception is poor, and cable is not in the future of anyone who cannot afford a satellite dish. Entertainment is therefore something that people invent, such as visiting, hunting, fishing, gardening, and the like. These people are largely out of touch with much of mainstream America, especially in terms of popular culture.

The school system consists of six schools. Two of these are modern, brick buildings in Snead Point, a K-8 elementary and a 9-12 high school, each with 26 teachers. The other four are very old indeed. One has six classrooms, and the rest have only four. Usually, more than one grade level is taught in each classroom in the small schools. Outside of town, each school is the largest building in the valley or pass in which it is located. At each of the five elementary schools, a Headstart center is attached, housed in a doublewide trailer.

Taylor's Run Elementary is a good example of the small schools. It is a four room school, with ducts and pipes exposed along the 12-foot high ceilings. Each classroom has nine-foot high windows running the length of the outside wall. The floors are tongue and groove hardwood, polished to a high sheen. Taylor's Run serves 125 students in its four classrooms, staffed by three teachers, one teaching principal, and a jack-of-all-trades custodian who fixes the old boiler, cooks breakfast and lunch, cleans the building, and runs the lost and found, among other things.

The building is spotlessly clean and decorated by the teachers and children. On my first visit, the Headstart teacher looked down the hall as the children changed classes and commented, "This is an example of what we called 'embattled pride' when I was a student up at Eastern. We don't have much, but we take care of what we've got."

Classroom practice in all these schools is based on state approved materials such as basal readers and other textbooks along with whatever the teachers will purchase out of their pockets. Problems are enormous. Children come from families so poor that they often come to school hungry and ill-clothed. Most parents can't read or write very well if at all, and often see little purpose in schooling for their children in a place that offers so few opportunities. The schools have none of the luxuries such as copying machines, laminating machines, or extra materials based on "room fees". It is subsistence schooling, limited in scope to one teacher, the state mandated texts, and little else. Many children have to struggle even to afford notebook paper and pencils.

Kaye White is a native of the county. She grew up in Snead Point and married her high school sweetheart. They love their home, the grandeur of the land and the freedom of life there, but they hate the poverty and ignorance. They attended the regional state university 90 miles away for undergraduate teacher education and then later, graduate degrees, he in administration and she in curriculum. After a number of years of experience in local schools, he was named principal of an elementary school, and she was a teacher in the high school. In so doing, they fulfilled a promise they had made each other, to return to Snead County from the university with the intellectual tools to help the people improve their lives. When her husband ran for and was elected superintendent, Kaye saw an opportunity for larger horizons for herself. Encouraged by her husband to write a grant proposal to fund a community school partnership program, she immediately set to work. Her proposal was approved.

Kaye's first thought was to conduct a formal survey of the needs of the county from the local inhabitants' perspectives. She was in many ways dismayed at what she found. Problems were endemic, with unemployment, poverty, and illiteracy most prominent. But much was favorable. Drug use had not made nearly the impact that it had in many places. Unlike the rest of the country, violence and crime were no worse than they had ever been. Many families were still intact nuclear and extended families with all the attendant benefits of mutual support that these provide. It was determined that children would be most benefited if parents could themselves go to school and improve their own education and family economics without destroying the fabric of local society. It was a mind numbing task. Kaye said:

> *It was hard to believe what I started with. Our dropout rate is 69% against a state rate of 26%. Our average educational level is seventh grade. We [the Parent Club] had trouble with eighth grade reading materials. I tried everything. We had an arts and crafts program. We tried a grandparents program and it failed. I did so much on my own time, I wound up in the hospital. It's good to talk to people who run other programs. We got to sharing ideas and I needed all of them. I can't believe how much paperwork I did last year. This year, I set some limits on what I do. I do two sessions a week at night. I make home visits, see Department of Human Services people, work with Appala-chian Work Services, and do my regular job of operating the Parents' Club during the school day.*

This kind of frontal assault soon consumed her. After a three-day stay in the hospital for exhaustion, she began to rethink how to proceed. She determined that helping the children meant helping parents. They, in turn, could not be helped by anything less than some sort of global solution. The parents needed to believe that their lives and those of their children could and would be better, so Kaye set out to find ways to accomplish this. For the fledgling Parents Clubs she was organizing, she selected a commercially available set of materials aimed at parenting skills. As stated, the parents had trouble with the literacy levels required, but she found ways to compensate. She knew that the best intentions flagged when nothing else changed in the parents lives. Hopelessness and iner-tia are difficult to overcome.

Several things needed to happen simultaneously. People obviously needed visible rewards for new ways of life. Kaye set out to broker some rewards. Her ideas began to gel as she became more and more involved in the lives of par-ents. Most of them knew they had poor literacy skills, so she recommend that they take pre-GED classes. Since no men ever came to any of Kaye's organiza-tions, she worked exclusively with mothers. Using her newest grant, the Dis-placed Homemaker Program, Kaye hired a retired teacher to prepare women to take the GED exam.

In talking to the director of the local Jobs Training Partnership Act office, she learned that the JTPA wished to place people in vocational training. They had been stymied to some degree by the low general level of education of most of their applicants. She held out hope of vocational training to her GED students, and things began to happen. Using JTPA money, arrangements were made to bus recent GED graduates down the mountain to the community college 80 miles away, thus overcoming the individual expense and trouble of attending. According to Kaye:

Our parents got some job skills and they took aptitude tests. We worked with managers at the plants for the ones that could be employed right now. Also we sent many to vocational school with grants which we worked to get for them. It doesn't cost the people a penny. We've got a bus and we buy them a sandwich for supper while they're over there. This is the toughest thing I have ever done, working with parents. You have to coax them along at their speed, not yours.

Problem solving has become second nature to Kaye. As her program evolves and changes, she continues to address the internal problems of the program and external problems of the parents, acting as an interface between the parents and available resources. For instance, when parents found the materials to be written at too high a reading level, Kaye contacted the author in an attempt to get them rewritten. When that did not work, she instituted cooperative reading at the meetings, using herself as the resource. The side effect of this practice has been noticeably better reading skills among the parents.

Kaye publicizes new opportunities to parents when they come to the club rooms to study for the GED or vocational training and in any other way she can think of. She networks relentlessly, seeking cooperative solutions to individual problems. She assesses and then problem solves.

My home visits were how I got the people out to start with. I just asked for a chance, told them to come to one meeting. I got parents' names at PTO meetings and went to visit them and then some of them referred me to other parents to share rides with and so on. . . . When a parent misses, I try to find out why. I don't pry into personal problems but maybe there is a problem with the program. I even bought a four wheel drive car for visits when [the weather] is bad.

Kaye was remarkably successful. Having started with virtually no interest from the community, she now has flourishing parent clubs in every elementary school in the county. In these clubs, she combines programs in innovative ways and offers a holistic response to the problems the parents bring to her. Unremitting networking and insistence that problems can be solved have led to participation in ways that were never foreseen. She said:

When I started, the teachers said these parents were only interested in what was in it for them . . . and the Headstart teachers were really surprised. The parents really came out and I had as many parents as I could handle. In times past, parents only came to school if they had to. This county can be a different world. These parents are not well educated here and we have to do what they need.

In the end, Kaye's programs all dovetailed to change the lives of children and parents forever. A number of persons have graduated from the medical technology program at the community college and are working as LPNs or medical techs and making more money than ever before in their lives. Others are working with other local employers now that they have the literacy skills to do so. And, the community college is training more.

In an average week, Kaye sees more than 100 parents, most of them poor, badly educated, and on welfare. And every week, she influences some of them to undertake life changing activities, bettering their parenting skills, improving their literacy, acquiring job training and new employment, and providing mutual support. In an area consisting of approximately 1200 households, positive change to so many of them upgrades the general level of life in the county for everybody.

FOUR CRITICAL COMPONENTS OF SUCCESSFUL PARENT/SCHOOL PARTNERSHIPS

The activities of these two individuals who have brought such positive change to so many others, are remarkably similar in spite of their quite different settings. However, the settings are remarkably similar upon closer observation, since all poor people share many of the same problems. By comparing these two individuals and their programs, four critical components emerge.

First, school/community partnership coordinators must occupy a recognized place in the hierarchy of their school systems. They are not volunteers, but persons who have a high level of legitimacy. And they are full-time coordinators whose success or failure depends on how well they meet the community's needs.

Second, program coordinators must be energetic, constantly innovative, and unremittingly positive. These two women brought agencies and people together who had never before conceived of cooperating. They communicated both verbally and in other ways to parents that they could have positive change in their lives. Likewise, they communicated to all sorts of other personnel and agencies that the parents were worth taking special pains over.

Third, program coordinators must be problem solvers by nature. Both Susan and Kaye solved problems over and over. They smoothed the way for everyone concerned all day, every day for service givers and consumers alike. A count of their personal contacts to either promote something or solve a problem culminates in an astonishing tally.

Finally, parents determined their own programmatic needs. Most parents in these situations felt little or no sense of ownership or pride in many aspects of their lives or in the education of their children. They embraced the parent club idea as an avenue to recognition and validation. They saw it as a chance to get something of value for themselves and for their children.

SUMMARY

In short, Kaye and Susan became the catalysts for change in their settings. To do this, they did whatever seemed necessary regardless of whether or not it was part of a job description. They gathered whatever was necessary. They persuaded whoever was needed. And they became whoever they needed to be: teacher, publicist, counselor, cheerleader, financier, chauffeur, home economist, or good-will ambassador. Susan changed the whole tenor of the Maryhurst School and, in doing so, changed lives and many aspects of the life in that community. Kaye, having driven thousands of miles from school to school, brought information and hope into isolated and otherwise abandoned homes. Both coordinators plugged into their communities quickly. They made home visits, and learned what the people wanted and needed. They sang songs, dressed up, held contests, and talked and talked to people who had, for the most part, no confidence in the beneficial effects of schooling or in the hope for positive change. In short, like the teachers in this book who took the children where they were, Kaye and Susan began by becoming part of the lives of parents.

Susan and Kaye demonstrated great faith and courage. They gathered support and resources from any and all available sources. They did not merely offer parenting skills classes and let it go at that. Rather, they chose instead to take responsibility for the outcomes of their programs. They got involved, expanded activities to meet problems, and enlisted people of all kinds into a common set of goals. This is extraordinary, and it presupposes coordinators who are not working to earn a living so much as they are working to live up to the standards they set for themselves. Both coordinators did well because they refused to do less. Find people like Kaye and Susan to organize it, and your parent-school partnership program can't fail.

References

Apppleton, D. (1938). *The community school*. New York: Century.

Cavarretta, J. (1998). Parents are a school's best friend. *Educational Leadership, 55*(8), 12-15.

Cohn-Vargas, B. & Grose, K. (1998). A partnership for literacy. *Educational Leadership, 55*(8), 45-48.

Fantini, M., Gittell, M., & Magat, R. (1970). How do we improve programs for parent involvement? *Educational Horizons, 66*(2), 58-59.

Kliebard, H. (1986). *The struggle for the American curriculum 1893-1958*. Boston: Routledge & Kegan Paul.

Mathews, D. (1997). The lack of a public for public schools. *Phi Delta Kappan, 78*(10), 740-743.

Wadsworth, D. (1997). Building a strategy for successful public engagement. *Phi Delta Kappan, 78*(10), 749-752.

Chapter 8

The Components of
Successful Literacy Instruction
in the Early Grades

Carole F. Stice and Nancy P. Bertrand

Several years ago, a local high school ESL teacher did something quite unusual. She took a year's leave of absence and spent every day with her daughter in Linda Edward's kindergarten classroom. Michelle didn't do that because she thought her daughter needed her in kindergarten. She did it because she wanted to watch how young children learn. She wanted to observe how they learn to read and write English in school within an informal classroom with a reflective, learner-centered teacher who espouses a constructivist philosophy. When the year was over, Michelle went back to her high school ESL classroom and set it up as a combination of a highly literate home and the kindergarten classroom she had just observed. She did that because she had seen for herself how to support the process of students' emergent and early developmental literacy.

This book was undertaken to allow a wider audience of prospective and in-service teachers access to that same wonderful kindergarten and five other equally powerful literacy and content rich, learner-centered classrooms. The contributors were asked to focus on their success stories with children at risk as examples of how reflective, learner-centered teachers help different children learn. They did that, and in the process we learned how they observe and come to know individual children, how they support the learning of all their students, how they build community, create curriculum, and view teaching and learning.

TEACHING AND LEARNING

In a recent article in the *Kappan*, "Sixty Years of Reading Research, but Who's Listening?", the authors cite an abundance of studies which support holistic, learner and literature-based, constructivist classrooms. These studies examined the development of children's reading, writing and thinking in a variety of situations, and their findings suggest that in the hands of knowledgeable teachers, and holistic, learner-centered classrooms produce equal or better results than traditional directed, teacher and/or materials-based classrooms (Zemelman, Daniels, & Bizar, 1999). As we have seen, knowledgeable teachers who believe in and support holistic, learner-centered classrooms are effective indeed.

But some teachers have claimed to be "holistic" when they haven't fully understood what changes in instruction such a position required. In another recent article in *The Reading Teacher*, Joyce (1999) laments the fact that too many educators and decision makers don't understand reading or writing and the complex nature of developmental literacy processes. And in many school systems, decisions are being made about what to teach and how to teach it by politicians rather than educators and scholars. Much of the knowledge generated about learning, human brains, language, and literacy achieved over the last half of this century is in danger of being lost. Half truths, as well as outright misinformation, are being promulgated as scientifically proven facts (Taylor, 1998).

According to Dahl, Scharer, Lawson, and Grogan (1999), for example, phonics instruction in whole language first grades, often characterized as informal, ad hoc, or minor and peripheral, is anything but. Rather, while whole language teachers rarely employ phonics workbooks or put children through a phonics skills "program" of some sort, upon close examination phonics instruction turns out to be substantial and extensive across the processes of both decoding and encoding.

The "great debate", according to Zemelman, Daniels, & Bizar (1999), isn't a clash between phonics and comprehension, or over what constitutes acceptable educational research. No thoughtful person could possibly believe that readers do not need phonic knowledge or that teachers refuse to provide it. No well meaning person would ever maintain that teachers purposefully teach children to misspell words or allow them to interpret text in illogical ways.

LITERACY

While there is genuine debate over how reading and writing instruction are best accomplished in schools, especially for children at risk, the majority of persons in the field today agree with Allington and Cunningham (1996). Reading and writing are meaning constructing activities, and the construction of meaning is only partly dependent on the individual words. Meaning, whether the learner is reading or writing, is also dependent on the context of the situation, the grammar in which the words are embedded, the learner's language and background knowledge, and how the learner's mind works.

Most educators also agree that sound and letter patterns are one of the systems that language uses to represent meaning. Therefore, phonemic awareness and phonemic segmentation are important to beginning reading, as well as crucial to spelling. But phonic knowledge is not the "cure all" it is frequently claimed to be (Allington, 1997). Young children who comprehend what they read do not need phonic drill and worksheet practice to improve their reading—they simply need to read from a wide variety of texts for a wide variety of purposes. However, those same children may need some specific phonics instruction as part of spelling during writing. While most proficient readers have extensive phonemic awareness, direct instruction in phonemic awareness and segmentation alone is not sufficient to create proficient readers. (Taylor, 1998).

There are as many paths to literacy as there are pathways into oral language. Literacy learning begins long before children enter school, long before they see their first workbook page or flash card. It begins in the learner's mind and in the learner's natural environment (Holdaway, 1979). This is true even for children of the very poor. We live in a literate society. Written language is everywhere. Everyone gets bills and junk mail. Everyone sees billboards along roadways, bread wrappers and cereal boxes at breakfast, the McDonalds down the street, the print on tee shirts, starter jackets, cans of soup, jars of peanut butter and bottles of COKE, as well as print on the cup from which they are drinking. While not all children are read to at home, virtually all children have television and other home and environmental literacy experiences.

It is the amount and nature of these early literacy experiences that affect how well and how quickly children learn to read (Delpit, 1986; Harste, Burke, & Woodward, 1983; Taylor, 1983; Teale, 1984). Events which demonstrate to children the many functions that print serves (e.g., writing lists, paying bills, ordering from catalogs, writing reminder notes, getting news and information from newspapers, receiving birthday cards, reading the church bulletin, comparing prices or ingredients of grocery items), together with early storybook reading, lay a successful foundation for school literacy. However, cultural imperatives strongly affect emergent literacy (Taylor & Dorsey-Gaines, 1988; Heath, 1983; Teale & Sulzby, 1989). The literature on children at risk suggests that when there is conflict between the expectations of school and the sociocultural mores of the community, learners often experience difficulty and may even reject their schooling (Dahl & Freppon, 1995; Donmoyer & Kos, 1993; Taylor & Dorsey-Gains, 1988).

WHAT TO DO?

The 1996 book, *Beginning to Read* by Marilyn Adams, was undertaken to provide guidance to teachers for teaching phonics as the foundation of beginning reading. Adams summarized and reported studies which found that phonemic awareness is one of the most important abilities leading to successful literacy development of young children. She concluded that learning phonics, i.e., learning to make those letter-to-sound, sound-to-letter correspondences is only one of the complex skills necessary for the development of proficient reading. And even though the book is a summary of studies about phonics, she reminds the reader early on that "however critical letter-to-sound correspondences may be, they are not enough. To become skillful readers, children need much more" (p. 29).

Indeed, skillful readers need to do much more than merely employ letter-to-sound relationships, and informed teachers need to understand the complexities of the reading process and reading development. Examine the reading of the following three children. These are all skillful readers for their ages. Look at what they are doing and what they have to know to be able to do what they do as readers.

The Carrot Seed

by Krauss (1945).

0101   *A little boy planted a carrot seed.*
0201   *His mother said, "I'm afraid it won't come up."*
0301   *His father said, "I'm afraid it won't come up."*
0401   *And his brother said, "It won't come up."*
0501   *Every day the little boy pulled up the weeds*
0502   *around the seed and sprinkled the ground with*
0503   *water. But nothing came up.*

In this selection, first-grader Jerome substitutes the word "corn" for "carrot". Why? Perhaps he knows about planting seeds and predicts the boy is planting a vegetable seed. He uses the initial letter and perhaps the double consonant in the middle to suggest which vegetable and substitutes one that makes sense. Then he reads "Andy", for "and". Maybe he expects the author to name the boy in the illustration. Next, he omits one of the instances of "up". Did he do that because he forgot what the word was? He read it correctly each of the other four times it occurred? No, he likely omitted it in that position because, unlike each of the other occurrences, the rules of English grammar do not require the preposition there. And finally, did Jerome's miscues interfere with his comprehension? His retelling revealed that he understood the story.

Clearly, the brains of proficient readers, whether children or adults, are actively engaged in making language and making sense. That is the reading process. Readers use letter-sound knowledge, knowledge about how words and grammar mean and work, and background knowledge from their own experiences to construct text during reading. They predict, self-correct, and think about what they are reading. Examine this next selection.

Miss Tizzy

by Gray (1993)

0101	*On Mondays, Miss Tizzy baked cookies.*
0201	*She let the neighborhood children put in the raisins, and then*
0202	*lick the bowl while the cookies were baking.*
0301	*The children loved it.*
0401	*On Tuesdays, Miss Tizzy made puppets out of old socks.*

Dolly, a lively third grader, does not read the names of the days of the week as plural until toward the end of the story. Why? She also omits the second instance of "the", not because she didn't know the word, but again, because of the rules of English. Every other occurrence of "the" is required, but the second "the" in front of the word raisins is not necessary. The sentence is perfectly grammatical and clear without it. Next, Dolly anticipates a parallel structure in the story when she reads "baked" for "made" in the 4th line (e.g., on Monday [she] baked cookies, on Tuesday [she] baked ___ . . .) As soon as Dolly sees the word "puppets" she realizes Miss Tizzy probably is not "baking" puppets. That doesn't make sense and she self-corrects. Both Frank Smith (1994), and Ken Goodman (1996), have explained the tricky nature of human perception by showing us how perception in reading is contextual and no different from our attempts to perceive any other events or objects in the world around us. As readers, we "see" what we think will be there.

Read this marked copy of a selection from a basal reader text.

A Place to Play

by Heller (1983)

0101	*"Look at this place," said Lin.*
0201	*"People can't play in it."*
0301	*"What can we do?" said Mark?. . . .*
0601	*"I can find Bill Downs," Tom told the boys and girls.*
0701	*"Bill Downs could help."*
0801	*"I can get Nan Green," said Pam*
0901	*"Nan Green could help."*
1001	*"We can get all the boys and girls to come," said Lin. . . .*
1301	*Nan Green came.*
1401	*Bill Downs came.*

Brian has made several miscues. However, a closer examination reveals not a poor reader, but a poorly crafted story. The structure of the text actually causes errors or miscues because some of what is there shouldn't be. The first illustration in the story shows a group of children looking at a trash filled park. Brian reads "here" for "in it", not because he doesn't know the words "in" and "it", but because children would be much more likely to say, "People can't play here", after seeing the picture, than "People can't play in it".

Brian's first self-correction occurs when he reads a question, but the dialogue carrier is "said" rather than "asked". As a skillful reader he also knows that once the author names a character the pronoun is supposed to be used until another name is mentioned. If the author renames the character, only the first name is needed unless there is some other reason to use both first and last names. Brian seems to be trying to make this text sound better than it is. But basal readers used to be written by formulas, and one of the rules was that the "new words" had to be used a certain number of times per story. The natural rules of literature were ignored and even proficient readers were often confused.

Proficient readers make errors precisely because they are engaged with making the text make sense rather than with just mechanically calling words. They predict and self-correct by using a variety of information sources. They apply what they know to help them perceive what the words are. They use the context, the grammar, and even the pictures if there are any. Proficient readers do not recognize words just by sounding out each word, and word recognition alone does not produce meaningful text or proficient readers. After all, word callers are people who read with few if any mistakes and frequently even with expression, but who do not understand what they read.

But English is a complex language and comprehension is not a simple or straight forward process. English consists of approximately sixteen vowel and twenty-eight consonant sounds. Its speech sounds are spelled with twenty-six letters for approximately 250 letter pattern combinations in words that would appear in elementary reading materials. For example, let's consider some of the ways long /a/ is spelled. Long /a/ is spelled:

a as in baby	*et as in bouquet*
ay as in day	*ei as in rein*
ai as in mail	*ea as in great*
a(silent e) as in cake	*ai(silent e) as in praise*
aigh as in straight	*ey as in they, and*
eigh as in neighbor	*ee as in matinee.*

These examples do not exhaust the possible spellings for the long /a/ sound, and they do not take into account dialect variations. The question is, when we are "teaching" phonics, whose dialect do we use, the dictionary, the teacher, the children, which children? After all, children from Boston to New Zealand who say "cah" for car will recognize c-a-r as the word meaning automobile regardless of how they pronounce it.

This leads directly to the problem of word identification when we read as opposed to correct spelling patterns when we write. The child who says "cah" for car may initially spell it kah, cah, caw, or any number of other options as they engage in hypothesizing about how that word is spelled based on what they know about letter-sounds and how they say the word. However, they soon learn the conventional spelling. But that doesn't end the difficulties. When we see, for example, one of the above long /a/ spelling patterns in print, will it always represent the long /a/ sound? The answer is no. Take the letter [a], but place it in the word father, the letter pattern [ai(silent e)], but place it in the word aisle, the letter pattern [ea], but in the word each. All of these combinations are spellings for long /a/—but not in those words. How do children ever develop into proficient spellers? Proficient spellers have good visual memory, and they develop several strategies for spelling new words.

Proficient readers also use more information than sound-letter patterns to identify words. And they know that merely recognizing words is not all they

must do to understand and interpret text. Consider the word "run". Easy to
identify, and pronounced more or less the same way throughout the country,
the word "run" has more than a dozen possible meanings: run in her stockings,
the salmon run, run to the store, the run on the bank, run the company, run for
congress, run for cover, run your mouth, run the water, run down, run over, run
the numbers, and so on. How is a reader to know? Readers' knowledge of language—of multiple word meanings as well as grammar—are all part of the
process. And words do not really even have meaning anyway until they are
embedded in grammar and context. Unfortunately, grammar is one aspect of
reading that many teachers ignore.

Take for example the two sentences, "The dog bit the boy", and "The boy
bit the dog". Even though they use the same five words, these two sentences
differ in meaning. The fact that the words are arranged differently means that
the "who-did-what-to-whom" relationship established by the grammar of the
two different strings of words is the information the reader must use in order to
make sense of these sentences. But word recognition and word order alone will
not yield successful reading because meaning is not built in a linear fashion,
through the identification of one word and its function, then the next word and
its function, and so on. Read the following example:

Mary had a little lamb . . .

Because we all share similar experiences, we naturally predict that *"it's
fleece was white as snow"* will be the next line. We also naturally think that the
proper noun and subject of the sentence "Mary" is a little girl, that the verb
"had" means "to own", and that the object "little lamb" refers to Mary's young
pet. However, if the next line is not *"it's fleece was white as snow, "* but:

. . . and she dropped mint jelly on her evening gown.

we must rethink the entire passage. As readers, we can't know the meanings of
the words in the first part until after having read the last part. Using our background knowledge and the sources of information that language provides, we
instantly reconstruct our understanding. "Mary" is actually a grown woman in
this context, "had" means "to eat" and "little lamb" refers to a small portion of
meat, not someone's pet. (Adapted from Edelsky, C., Altwerger, B., & Flores,
B.,1991.) It takes much longer to describe what proficient readers do than it
does for them to do it.

As with word identification, sentence processing alone is not sufficient to
understand and interpret text. Sentences may make sense and be perfectly grammatical and still not be "understood". That is, comprehending is not merely a
matter of grappling with the grammar and word meanings of each individual

sentence. For example, the same exact sentence can have two entirely different meanings. "What about that arm?" is a simple question most second-graders could "read". But, it has virtually no meaning separated from its context which tells what or to whom the arm belongs. Is it the arm of a pitcher in an exciting story about the last game of a world series? Perhaps it is the arm of a sofa in a mystery story where the villain is searching for a hidden map. Or maybe it refers to an alien monster's surviving appendage writhing on the floor in the science lab of a space ship.

Another example can be seen in the use of personal references. When pronouns are used to refer to several persons in a story, typically in the form of dialogue, potential confusion arises. For instance, "*They* told *me you* had gone to see *her* and that *you* talked about *me*. *I* want to know what *you* said and what *she* is going to tell *him*." Only the context of the event and the information carried in the head of the reader from across previous parts of the story makes this conversation intelligible. While the potential for difficulty is present, this is not a complicated strand. If it is embedded in a real text, it is quite easy to track and comprehend.

Armed with such knowledge about what reading really is, how long will we allow non-educators to define reading and try to tell us how to teach it? How long can we keep silent when non-educators, from psychologists to politicians, tell the public that reading is merely a matter of sounding out words? Reading is the active, constructive process of making sense of text. Reading is first and foremost about using what we know to make text meaningful. As with all other forms of human perception, proficient readers perceive what they think will be there based on context and prior knowledge. They use their sense of language (including phonic knowledge), and their knowledge of what is reasonable in the world to self-correct what is not meaningful. Simply identifying the words correctly is not reading. Besides, as we have seen, words have meaning only as they are embedded in language anyway.

An examination of real readers reading real text reveals that they (we), all make mistakes or miscues exactly because they (we) are interacting with the language and ideas presented. Since reading is not simply a matter of getting all the words articulated correctly, if we teach it as though it were, we create unnecessary problems for learners.

If reading is so complex, how do kids ever do it? They do it because language learning is natural for human beings. But which programs are best for handling all the complexities of literacy development? According to research, there are no materials that adequately program students into literacy. The key is not which program you use, but what the teacher knows about reading and writing, and how these processes develop in young children. The teacher must become the program! When that occurs, most any materials may be success-fully employed as resources.

WHAT TEACHERS MUST KNOW AND DO

Classroom curriculum can typically be identified as one of three types: learner-centered, teacher-centered, or materials-centered. Most classrooms are materials-centered. Teachers base instruction on the textbooks provided. That is probably the way you remember being taught and the way many teachers were, and still are, trained to teach. Since there are no materials which ad-equately do the job, part of the problem with learner achievement in early lit-eracy is the over abundance of materials-driven classrooms. Learner-centered classrooms are different. They are places where teachers use authentic assess-ment and learner interests to plan instruction and develop curriculum. In these classrooms teachers may integrate subjects, employ portfolio assessment, and engage students in cooperative groups, inquiry projects, and hands-on learning of various types.

The classrooms described in this book are learner-centered. They are taught by informed, reflective teachers. These teachers do not employ materials that structure the curriculum for them. They do not follow arbitrary curriculum guides, predetermined lesson plans, and someone else's idea of what their stu-dents need. They do not employ "cute" activities for their students, use an abun-dance of black line ditto masters, or teach to tests. Rather, they understand child development, learning, the nature of reading and writing, and the nature of the learning to read and write process. They study their students to deter-mine their capabilities, what skills and strategies, strengths and needs they have, and what interests them as they are learning to read and write. Their focus is helping their students become independent learners and to think like readers and writers.

To assist teachers in learning what they need to know and in clearing up current misinformation, the Northwest Regional Educational Laboratories, the National Council of Teachers of English, and the International Reading Asso-ciation have published jointly a document on beginning literacy. This synthesis of what teachers of young children need to understand, believe, and do in order to successfully teach developmental reading and writing goes beyond the me-chanical aspects of language processing (i.e. letter/sound relationships, decod-ing words, conventional spelling, and making attractive letters on paper). En-titled *Building a Knowledge Base in Reading* (Braunger & Lewis, 1997), this book was designed for teachers, policy-makers, and other interested persons.

According to *Building a Knowledge Base in Reading*, teachers must understand many things, including that reading is constructing meaning from text. They must understand what it means when we say that reading is an active, cognitive, and affective process in which readers utilize their background knowledge and employ predicting and self-correcting. They must understand what it means when we say that proficient readers use meaning, structural cues, and sound-letter patterns simultaneously as they read. They must know how to help young children learn to do that.

This synthesis of what teachers need to know and do suggests that in order to help children develop the complex interaction of skills and strategies they must use as proficient readers, teachers should know, among other things, that social interaction is essential in learning to read and write. Cathy's third graders read and engaged in integrated units. They read about and researched their own topics within broader classroom themes. They created their own alphabet and counting books, sharing them with the kindergartners in their school. They developed celebrations, rituals and ceremonies because Cathy understands that social interaction and self-confidence are essential keys to successful literacy learning, and that reading and writing develop together.

Also, according to Braunger & Lewis (1997), reading and writing involve complex thinking. We can see that in practice as we read about how John worked with his learning disabled fourth graders; as he invited Kent to read an advanced chapter book with him so he could scaffold reading strategies and word knowledge onto what Kent already knew. Reading and writing involve complex thinking. Literacy learning requires environments rich in literacy experiences, resources, and where the available models facilitate reading and writing development. Engagement in reading and writing are central to successful learning. Melanie's inner-city second-graders were immersed in rich literacy experiences. They read good books and wrote to their favorite authors. They wrote stories and shared their writing with each other because Melanie knows children need to learn successful reading and writing strategies in the context of real reading and real writing. She realizes that children's understandings of print are not the same as adult understandings, and she urges her students to explore in ways that support their growing understanding.

In addition, the Braunger & Lewis (1997) study found that children learn best when teachers employ a variety of ways to demonstrate how prior knowledge is utilized in both reading and writing. Tina's children negotiated meaning together and took ownership of their classroom. They wrote about their lives and shared these products because she values the background knowledge and prior experiences of her students, knowing that these are critical to growth in reading and writing. Children need ample opportunities to read, read, read, and to write, write, write (as well as talk, talk, talk, and think, think, think). Teachers need to monitor and guide the development of reading and writing processes if they are to achieve student success.

Linda's kindergarten classroom is awash in opportunities for the children to engage in reading and writing. It provides many daily demonstrations of literacy and employs ample models of both decoding and encoding of sound-letter associations in print that the children know and can read. Linda does these things because she knows that young children's understanding of print, their phonemic awareness, phonics knowledge and emergent literacy develop through a variety of reading and writing opportunities and models.

A look into Kathy's multi-age ESL classroom also reveals an environment rich in literacy experiences, resources, and models that facilitate reading development. In addition, we see abundant evidence of students reading good books and using those books as models for their own language development, their writing, game playing, and learning. Kathy's students, as the students described in this book, have available to them a rich array of literature, teacher explanations and demonstrations, and access to a wide variety of responsive language interactions.

These research-based, core understandings are what teachers and classrooms must provide so that young children have the best foundation possible from which to ultimately reach their full literacy potentials. The teachers whose classrooms you have just encountered apply these understandings because they know that children need time, texts and other resources. They are themselves knowledgeable, supportive teachers who demonstrate, explain, model, encourage, praise, point out, suggest, question, and mentor their students into literacy. They know that children need to develop inner control over their own reading and writing processes and that such control develops best in print and content rich classrooms where students feel accepted and at least partly in charge.

We see examples of all that and more in each of these classrooms. But beyond that, these teachers teach with enthusiasm and caring. They are teachers who are genuinely interested in children, in how they learn, develop and grow. They help their students develop confidence in themselves and in their ability to learn. They are innovators, and since innovation usually changes the classroom into something considerably different from what parents remember, they also spend considerable time explaining what they do and why they do it. They explain and reassure parents and principals, adapting to what parents and principals want when they can do so without violating their own beliefs and experiences.

WHAT TEACHERS SHOULD AVOID

In addition to providing a detailed research base describing what teachers of young children need to know and do, Braunger & Lewis (1997), also provide a rather succinct list of instructional practices that seem to hinder full literacy development. Practices to avoid include relying solely on prepackaged programs or textbooks, teaching to standardized tests, emphasizing phonics only, using workbooks and pre-made ditto sheets for drilling students on isolated skills, employing sets of comprehension questions rather than engaging students in discussions of good books, using preset lesson plans focused on a teaching letters one at a time and "sight words", insisting on correctness in early oral reading and thereby making perfect oral reading the goal of reading instruction rather than interpretation and comprehension, expecting students to spell correctly all the words they can read, and requiring, for the major part of the school day, that young children be quiet and do their own "work".

We know that reading and writing achievement are directly related to the amount of reading, writing, and talking about books in which learners engage. We know how to cause children to love or hate reading and writing. We know how to teach children to simply call words or to construct meaning and develop inner control over these processes for themselves. We know that reading and writing should develop together, that teacher attitudes and children's access to high quality resources are among the most significant of keys to early success. Independence in reading and writing is the goal, and to that end, teachers engage learners in guided instruction, reading with them, and talking about books. And talking about books motivates children to read as well as enhances the development of other important cognitive strategies. In fact, classroom studies are showing that social interaction, as well as guided strategy instruction (i.e. showing children how to do what proficient readers and writers do) are strongly related to success in learning to read and write in the early grades (Guthrie, Schafer, Wang, & Afflerbach, 1995).

Effective classrooms such as the ones you encountered in this book are based on these core principles. Many of the students in such classrooms, while entering with some at-risk characteristics, soon begin to like school and to think in literate ways. They grow in self-confidence and come to view themselves as competent. The classrooms in this book represent hundreds of wonderful literacy and content rich, learner-centered classrooms taught by knowledgeable, reflective, enthusiastic and caring teachers.

All of us, teachers, administrators, *and parents* must search out our own powerful examples of reflective, learner-centered, literacy rich classrooms in their own schools; learn about them, learn from them, and find ways to help new teachers emulate them as much as possible. And society must recognize the need to protect and defend good teachers and their classrooms (Goodman, 1998), from unnecessary and misguided control by politicians and bureaucrats— for these classrooms are all endangered species. If they disappear, what will take their place?

References

Adams, M. (1996). *Beginning to read: Thinking and learning about print.* Cambridge, MA: MIT Press.

Allington, R. (1997).Overselling phonics. *Reading World, 15* (1),15–16.

Allington, R., & Cunningham, P. (1996). *Schools that work.* New York, NY: Harper Colins.

Baumann, J., & Duffy, A. (1997). *Engaged reading for pleasure and learning: A report from the national reading research center.* Athens, GA: University of Georgia Press.

Braunger, J., & Lewis, J. (1997). *Building a knowledge base in reading.* Portland, OR: Co-published by Northwest Regional Education Laboratory's Curriculum and Instruction Services, National Council of Teachers of English, & International Reading Association.

Bruner, J. & Cole, M. (1990). *Early literacy: Developing child.* Cambridge, MA: Harvard University Press.

Cambourne, B. & Turbil, J. (1987). *Coping with chaos.* Portsmouth, NH: Heinemann.

Clay, M. (1991). *Becoming literate.* Portsmouth, NH: Heinemann.

Dahl, K., Scharer, P., Lawson, L., & Grogan, P. (1999). *Phonics teaching and learning in whole language first grade classrooms.* Final Report for the Office of Educational Research and Improvement. No. R305F60180.Columbus, OH: The Ohio State University Press.

Delpit, L. (1986). Skills and other dilemmas of a progressive Black educator. *Harvard Educational Review*, 56, 379–385.

Donmoyer, R. & Kos, R. (1993). At-risk students: Insights from/about research. In R. Donmoyer & R. Kos (Eds.), *At-risk students: Portraits, policies, programs, and practices* (7–36), Albany, NY: SUNY Press.

Edelsky, C., Altwerger, B., & Flores, B. (1991). *Whole language: What's the difference?* Portsmouth, NH: Heinemann.

Fountas, I., & Pinnell, G. (1996). *Guided reading: Good first teaching.* Portsmouth, NH: Heinemann.

Goodman, K. (1996). *On Reading.* Portsmouth, NH: Heinemann.

Goodman, K. (1998) (Ed.), *In defense of good teaching: What teachers need to know about the "reading wars".* York, ME: Stenhouse. Publishers.

Goodman, Y. (Ed.) (1990). *How children construct literacy: Piagetian Perspectives.* Newark, DE: IRA.

Graves, D. (1995). *A fresh look at writing.* Portsmouth, NH:Heinemann.

Gray, L. (1993). *Miss Tizzy.* New York, NY: Simon & Schuster.

Guthrie, J., Schafer, W., Wang, Y., & Afflerbach, P. (1995). Relationships of instruction to amount of reading: An exploration of social, cognitive, & instructional connections. *Reading Research Quarterly, 30* (1),8–25.

Harste, J., Burke, C., & Woodward, V. (1983). The young child as reader-writer, and informant. (Grant No. NIE-G–80–0121.) Washington, DC: National Institute of Education.

Heath, S.B. (1983). *Ways with words: Language, life, and work in communities and classrooms.* New York: Cambridge University Press.

Joyce, B. R. (1999). Reading about reading: Notes from a consumer to the scholars of literacy. *The Reading Teacher.* 52 (7), 662–671.

Heller, D.(1983). "A place to play." *Hang on to your hats.* Glenview, IL: Scott Foresman, 8–10.

Holdaway, D.(1979). *Foundations of literacy.* Toronto:Scholastic-TAB.

Krauss, R. (1945). *The carrot seed.* New York: HarperCollins.

National Center for Educational Statistics, (1993). *Executive summary of the NAEP report card for the nation and the states.* Washington, DC: Prepared by the Educational Testing Service under contract with the National Center for Educational Statistics and the Office of Educational Research and Improvement of the U.S. D. O. E.

Smith, F. (1994) *Understanding Reading, 5th ed.* Hillsdale, New Jersey: Lawrence Erlbaum.

Taylor, D. (1983). *Family literacy: Young children's learning to read and write.* Portsmouth, NH: Heinemann.

Taylor, D., & Dorsey-Gaines, C. (1988). *Growing-up literate: Learning from inner-city families.* Portsmouth, NH: Heinemann.

Taylor, D. (1998). *Beginning to read and the spin doctors of science: The political campaign to change America's mind about how children learn to read.* Urbana, IL: NCTE

Teale, W. (1984). Reading to young children: Its significance for literacy development. In H. Goelman, A. Oberg. & F. Smith (Eds.), *Awakening to literacy*. (110–121). London: Heinemann.

Teale, W. & Sulzby, E. (1989). *Emergent literacy: Writing and reading.* Norwood, NJ: Ablex.

Zemelman, S., Daniels, H., & Bizar, M. (March, 1999), Sixty years of Reading research—but who's listening? *Phi Delta Kappan.* 80 (3), 513–517.

Suggested Professional Readings in Both Early Literacy and Children At Risk

Adams, M. (1996). *Beginning to read: Thinking and learning about print*. Cambridge, MA: MIT Press.

Allington, R. (1997). Overselling phonics. *Reading world.15*(1), 15-16.

Allington, R., & Cunningham, P. (1996). *Schools that work*. New York, NY: Harper Collins.

Barron, M. (1990). *I learned to read and write the way I learned to talk*. Katonah, NY: Richard C. Owen.

Baumann, J., & Duffy, A. (1997). *Engaged reading for pleasure and learning: A report from the national reading research center*. Athens, GA: University of Georgia Press.

Bissex, G. (1980). *Gyns at Wrk: A Child learns to read and write*. Cambridge, MA: Harvard University Press.

Bolton, F., & Snowball, D. (1993). *Teaching spelling: A Practical Resource*. Portsmouth, NH: Heinemann.

Braunger, J., & Lewis, J. (1997). *Building a knowledge base in reading*. Portland, OR: Co-published by Northwest Regional Education Laboratory's Curriculum and Instruction Services, National Council of Teachers of English, & International Reading Association.

Bruner, J. & Cole, M. (1990). *Early literacy: Developing child*. Cambridge, MA: Harvard University Press.

Bruner, J. (1986). *Actual minds, possible worlds*. Cambridge, MA: Harvard University Press.

Butler, A. & Turbil, J. (1984). *Toward a reading/writing classroom*. Portsmouth, NH: Heinemann.

Calkins, L. (1983). *Lessons from a child*. Portsmouth, NH: Heinemann.

Calkins, L. (1986). *The art of teaching writing,* (2nd ed.) Portsmouth, NH: Heinemann.

Calkins, L. & Harwayne, S. (1991). *Living between the lines*. Portsmouth, NH: Heinemann.

Cambourne, B. (1988). *The whole story*. Toronto: Scholastic-TAB.

Cambourne, B., & Turbill, J. (1995). *Responsive evaluation*. Portsmouth, NH: Heinemann.

Cambourne, B. & Turbill, J. (1987). *Coping with chaos*. Portsmouth, NH: Heinemann.

Clay, M. (1975). *What did I write?* Portsmouth, NH: Heinemann.

Clay, M. (1991). *Becoming literate: The construction of inner control*. Portsmouth, NH: Heinemann.

Cochran-Smith, M. (1984).*The making of a reader*. Norwood, NJ: Ablex.

Cullinan, B. (1987). *Children's literature and the reading program*. Newark, DE: IRA.

Delpit, L. (1986). Skills and other dilemmas of a progressive Black educator. *Harvard Educational Review*, 56, 379-385.

Donmoyer, R. & Kos, R. (1993). At-risk students: Insights from/about research. In R. Donmoyer & R. Kos (Eds.), *At-Risk Students: Portraits, policies, programs, and practices* (7-36), Albany, NY: SUNY Press.

Duckworth, E. (1987). *The having of wonderful ideas and other essays on teaching and learning*. New York: Teachers College Press.

Dyson, A. (1989). *Multiple worlds of child writers: Friends learning to write*. New York: Teachers College Press.

Ernst, K. (1993). *Picturing learning: Artists and writers in the classroom*. Portsmouth, NH: Heinemann.

Ferriero, E. & Teberosky, A. (1982). *Literacy before schooling*. Portsmouth, NH: Heinemann.

Fountas, I., & Pinnell, G. (1996). *Guided reading: Good first teaching*. Portsmouth, NH: Heinemann.

Gentry, R. (1987). *Spel... is a four letter word*. Portsmouth, NH: Heinemann.

Goodman, K. (1996). *In defense of good teaching*. Portsmouth, NH: Heinemann.

Goodman, K. (1997). *On reading*. Portsmouth, NH: Heinemann.

Goodman, Y. (Ed.) (1990). *How children construct literacy: Piagetian perspectives*. Newark, DE: IRA.

Goodman, Y., Watson, D., & Burke, C. (1987). *Reading miscue inventory: Alternative procedures*. Katonah, NY: Richard C. Owen.

Graves, D. (1995). *A fresh look at writing*. Portsmouth, NH: Heinemann.

Graves, D. (1982). *Writing: Teachers and children at work*. Portsmouth, NH: Heinemann.

Graves, D. (1989). *Experiment with fiction*. Portsmouth, NH: Heinemann.

Graves, D. (1991). *Build a literate classroom*. Portsmouth, NH: Heinemann.

Graves, D. 1989). *Investigate non-fiction*. Portsmouth, NH: Heinemann.

Harste, J., Woodward, V. & Burke, C. (1984). *Language stories and literacy lessons*. Portsmouth, NH: Heinemann.

Hickman, J. & Cullinan, B. (1989). *Children's literature in the classroom: Weaving Charlotte's web*. Norwood, MA: Christopher-Gordon.

Hill, S. & Hill, T. (1990). *The collaborative classroom*. Portsmouth, NH: Heinemann.

Holdaway, D. (1979). *Foundations of literacy*. Toronto:Scholastic-TAB.

Johnson, P. (1992). *A book of one's own: Developing literacy through making books*. Portsmouth, NH: Heinemann.

Lyons, C., Pinnell, G., DeFord, D. (1993). *Partners in learning: Teachers and children in reading recovery*. New York: Teachers College Press.

Meek, M. (1986). *Learning to read*. Portsmouth, NH: Heinemann.

Mooney, M. (1990). *Reading to, with, and by*. Katonah, NY: Richard C. Owen.

Olson, J. (1992). *Envisioning writing: Toward an integration of drawing and writing*. Portsmouth, NH: Heinemann.

Pappas, C., Kieffer, B. & Levstik, L. (1990). *An integrated language arts perspective in the elementary school*. White Plains, NY: Longman.

Peterson, R. (1992). *Life in a crowded place: Making a learning community*. Portsmouth, NH: Heinemann.

Peterson, R. & Eeds, M. (1990). *Grand conversation: Literature groups in action*. Jefferson City, MO: Scholastic.

Rhodes, L., & Shanklin, N. (1993). *Windows into literacy: Assessing learners K-8*. Portsmouth, NH: Heinemann.

Routman, R. (1991). *Invitations*. Portsmouth, NH: Heinemann.

Roy, S., & Steele, J. (1986). *Young imagination: Writing and artwork by children of New South Wales*. Portsmouth, NH: Heinemann.

Short, K., & Harste, J. (1996). *Creating classrooms for authors and inquirers*. Portsmouth, NH: Heinemann.

Short, K. & Pierce, K. (1990). *Talking about books: Creating literate communities*. Portsmouth, NH: Heinemann.

Smith, F. (1988). *Joining the Literacy Club*. Portsmouth, NH: Heinemann.

Stephens, D. (1990). *What matters? A primer for teaching reading*. Portsmouth, NH: Heinemann.

Stires, S. (Ed.) (1991). *With promise: Redifining reading and writing for special students*. Portsmouth, NH: Heinemann.

Taylor, D. (1983). *Family literacy: Young children's learning to read and write*. Portsmouth, NH: Heinemann.

Taylor, D., & Dorsey-Gaines, C. (1988). *Growing-up literate: Learning from inner-city families*. Portsmouth, NH: Heinemann.

Taylor, D. (1998). *Beginning to read and the spin doctors of science: The political campaign to change America's mind about how children learn to read*. Urbana, IL: NCTE

Teale, W. (1984). Reading to young children: Its significance for literacy development. In H. Goelman, A. Oberg. & F. Smith (Eds.), *Awakening to literacy*. (110-121). London: Heinemann.

Teale, W. & Sulzby, E. (1989). *Emergent literacy: Writing and reading*. Norwood, NJ: Ablex.

Temple, C., Nathan, R. & Burris, N. (1982). *The beginnings of writing*. Boston: Allyn & Bacon.

Tierney, R., Carter, M., & Desai, L. (1991). *Portfolio assessment and the reading-writing classroom*. Norwood, MA: Christopher-Gordon.

Trelease, J. (1995). *The new read-aloud handbook*. New York: Viking/Penguin.

Turbill, J. (1982). *No better way to teach writing*. Portsmouth, NH: Heinemann.

Walsh, H. *Social studies and the young learner*. Washington, DC: National Council for the Social Studies.

Wells, G. (1986). *The meaning makers*. Portsmouth, NH: Heinemann.

Wells, G., & Chang-Wells, G. (1992). *Constructing knowledge together: Classrooms as centers of inquiry and literacy*. Portsmouth, NH: Heinemann.

Wilde, S. (1991). *You kan red this! Spelling and punctuation for whole language classrooms, K-6.* Portsmouth, NH: Heinemann.

Zemelman, S., Daniels, H., & Bizar, M. (1999), Sixty years of Reading research—but who's listening? *Phi Delta Kappan.* 80 (3), 513-517.

Index

Editors

John E. Bertrand is a native of North Carolina, though he has lived most of his life in Tennessee. He received his Ph.D. from The Ohio State University in Research and Curriculum in 1986. He has worked as an elementary and middle school teacher, football and basketball coach, director of an alternative school for troubled youth, a full time researcher, and teaching professor. Recently retired from Tennessee State University, he is now a full time writer. He lives on a farm in Readyville, Tennessee, with his wife, Nancy, their daughter, Jenny, and a plethora of animals. His previous works include co-authorship of Integrating Reading and the Other Language Arts and co-editorship of Empowering Children at Risk of School Failure.

Carole F. Stice is professor of Reading and Language Arts Education at Tennessee State University in Nashville, Tennessee, where she was named Researcher of the Year in 1992 and Teach of the Year in 1995. A graduate of Florida State University, she received her Ph.D. in Elementary Reading and Language Arts Education in 1974. Carole is an active member of the Tennessee Education Community. She sponsors the local TAWL group, serves on the editorial board for the journal of the Tennessee Reading Association to which she contributes an instructional strategy lesson for each issue. Carole is the co-author of *Integrating Reading and Language Arts,* a textbook published by Wadsworth, *Reading for Adults,* a series of guided readers for adults published by NTC/Contemporary Books, and several information books with websites for adolescents soon to be published by The Wright Group.

Contributors

Nancy Bertrand is a professor of Elementary Special Education at Middle Tennessee State University. She received her Ph.D. in Early and Middle Childhood Education at The Ohio State University, and was the recipient of the Kappa Delta Pi award for Educational Leadership in 1990. Presently, Dr. Bertrand serves as the chairperson for the Tennessee Reading Association "Celebrate Literacy Awards" Program, which recognizes Tennessee's young authors in grades K-12. An active member of many educational societies. she has presented several articles about whole language and at-risk children at major conferences and co-authored the book *Integrating Reading and the Other Language Arts: Foundations of a Whole Language Curriculum* (1994) published by Wadsworth Publishing Co.

Cathy Clarkson happily teaches 3rd grade at Johnson Elementary in the Franklin Special School District in Franklin, Tennessee. Cathy got her teaching degree at Belmont University and her Master's degree at Tennessee State University. She enjoys playing music with her husband, Bill, and other teachers in a group they call Pick'n'Spin. Her Two children, Sam and Lily, keep her learning about the joys of children.

Tina De Stephen is a 2nd grade teacher at Walnut Grove School in the city of Franklin, Tennessee. She graduated Magna Cum Laude from San Francisco State University, and has taught in California, New Mexico, and rural Tennessee. As a recipient of a National Council of Teachers of English (NCTE) research grant, Ms. De Stephen completed "A Study of the Effect of all Expanded Field Trip Program on the Written Development of Rural Pre-First Children." She was president of Teachers Applying Whole Language (TAWL) of Middle Tennessee and served as a delegate to the Citizen Ambassador Program for Children's Literature and Language Arts in China. She was honored as a fellow by the James R. Stokely Institute at the University of Tennessee, Knoxville. She received the Career Ladder III award from the Tennessee Department of Education. An active presenter at numerous district, regional, and national workshops and conferences, she was a consultant on whole language at the summer Training Institute for teachers of Choctaw students in Philadelphia, Mississippi.

Linda Edwards teaches kindergarten at Brookmeade Elementary School in Nashville, Tennessee. She is especially interested in early literacy development and enjoys sharing her expertise with colleagues at conferences and occasionally as a freelance consultant.

Kathy Miller is the Director of the ESL programs at the McFadden School in Murfreefboro, Tennessee, where she has taught for 8 years. She received her B.S. from Belmont University in Nashville, and has completed more than 25 hours of graduate credits. An elementary school teacher for 15 years, she has taught in both Georgia and Texas. She is a member of the International Reading Association.

Melanie Ricks is a former 2/3rd grade teacher with the Nashville, Davidson County, Metropolitan School System. Melanie taught grades 2 & 3 for 11 years. She completed her M.A. in Education several years ago, has been named teacher of the year by her school, and has achieved the highest ranking on Career Ladder this state awards. She has made numerous presentations to local and regional Teacher and parent groups as well as school faculties. In 1994, she began training as a leader for the Center for Innovation in Education's program "Math . . . A Way of Thinking." Melanie is also a Reading Recovery teacher and currently teaching 1st grade in Nashville.